POLICE
DISASTER
OPERATIONS

POLICE
DISASTER
OPERATIONS

By

ALLEN P. BRISTOW
Professor of Police Administration
California State College
Los Angeles, California

CHARLES C THOMAS • PUBLISHER
Springfield • *Illinois* • *U.S.A.*

Published and Distributed Throughout the World by

CHARLES C THOMAS • PUBLISHER
BANNERSTONE HOUSE
301-327 East Lawrence Avenue, Springfield, Illinois, U.S.A.
NATCHEZ PLANTATION HOUSE
735 North Atlantic Boulevard, Fort Lauderdale, Florida, U.S.A.

This book is protected by copyright. No part of it may be reproduced in any manner without written permission from the publisher.

© 1972, by CHARLES C THOMAS • PUBLISHER
ISBN 0-398-02244-5 (cloth)
ISBN 0-398-02481-2 (paper)
Library of Congress Catalog Card Number: 75-184592

With THOMAS BOOKS *careful attention is given to all details of manufacturing and design. It is the Publisher's desire to present books that are satisfactory as to their physical qualities and artistic possibilities and appropriate for their particular use.* THOMAS BOOKS *will be true to those laws of quality that assure a good name and good will.*

Printed in the United States of America
JJ-1

CONTENTS

Chapter *Page*

1. Introduction 3
2. Disaster Role of the Police 7
3. Police Disaster Planning 16
4. Disaster Management 44
5. Disaster Psychology 78
6. What the Police Disaster Commander Should Know About Common Disasters 89
7. Disaster Case Studies 131

Appendix

A. California Mutual Aid Plan 159
B. A Mutual Aid Agreement 171
C. Model Organization and Function Plan 179
D. Plan for Change of Function During a Disaster .. 183
E. Simulation Games 184
F. Model Disaster Response Plan 201
G. Disaster Response Simulations 204
H. Emergency Control Center Model 215
I. Disaster Log Example 219
J. Pollution Alert System 224

Index 227

POLICE
DISASTER
OPERATIONS

1
INTRODUCTION

Several terms should be clarified which indicate the scope and content of this book. The purpose for which it was written should also be of interest to the reader and will explain why some subjects are stressed while others may receive little attention.

DEFINITION OF TERMS

Disaster

Dictionaries refer to a disaster as a happening which may cause great damage or create a calamity, which in turn is defined as a misfortune. Sociologists define a disaster as a collective stress situation. They feel that such a situation occurs where large numbers of a given population are deprived of their normal or expected life conditions. One large insurance corporation defines a major disaster as an incident wherein twenty-five or more people are killed. They classify a situation in which five or more people are killed as a catastrophe. This company does not include monetary loss in their definition. Others find it necessary to define the term disaster for control or reporting purposes who further classify by magnitude, speed of onset, duration and area or population affected. In such definitions disasters may be referred to as being of the first magnitude or second magnitude.

For purposes of defining the term disaster with respect to its use in this book the following will probably be most practical:

> Any incident, excluding mass law violation (demonstrations or riots) which requires a law enforcement agency to completely exhaust its physical resources to protect life and property.

The reader may wonder why demonstrations and riots were excluded from the definition. Incidents of mass law violation, such as acts of civil disobedience or riots, at first may appear to be similar to the hazards affecting a community during a disaster—

yet there are some basic differences. Police riot and demonstration operations are largely concerned with control and prevention of misbehavior, gathering of evidence, making arrests, preparing cases for prosecution, and the protection of the constitutional rights of those involved. The police role in disaster operations is rarely concerned with these aspects. Disaster operations cast the police in an assistance role, protecting life and property.

Police

This term refers to the law enforcement agency in whose primary jurisdiction a disaster has occurred. It may be a city police department, a county sheriff's office, or a state highway patrol. It is acknowledged that a wide variety of other agencies are involved in disaster operations: Civil Defense, Salvation Army, Red Cross, etc. However, police disaster operations are so different in nature and scope that they may be separated from the activities of other community based organizations.

From time to time in this book, techniques may be suggested which the reader may identify in his jurisdiction as being the responsibility of the fire service. So be it. Our country is unique in that from community to community the separation of duties among the protective services may differ.

EXAMPLES

Following are a number of examples which tend to illustrate the wide range of incidents which constitute a disaster under the author's definition.

> Hartford, Conn.—July, 1944. A circus tent fire killed 168 persons and injured countless others. Police were involved with panic control, evacuation, crowd control, convergence control, prevention of looting, body recovery, and destruction of escaped wild animals.
>
> Vicksburg, Miss.—Dec., 1953. A tornado killed 38, injured 270, and created damage estimated at 25 million dollars. Police were involved in cordoning the area, searching for bodies in debris, recovery and identification of the dead, prevention of looting, and providing ambulance transportation for the injured.

Introduction

Hilo, Hawaii—Feb., 1955. An eruption of the Puna volcano required extensive emergency evacuation and relocation of residents; and the duration of the incident coupled with the tourist nature of the location required extensive convergence control.

Elizabethport, New Jersey—Sept., 1958. A train wreck killed 48 and injured countless others. Police were involved in emergency traffic control, recovery of the dead, insuring rapid transportation of the injured, and prevention of looting.

Indianapolis, Ind.—Oct., 1963. An explosion in the coliseum killed 73 and injured 381. Police were involved with panic prevention, crowd control, convergence control, body recovery, identification of the dead, provision of rapid transportation of the injured, and prevention of looting.

Los Angeles, Calif.—Dec., 1963. The Baldwin Hills reservoir collapse required police to evacuate thousands of residents from the path of the flood waters within 1½ hours, set up looting control of evacuation area, and prevent re-entry.

Crescent City, Calif.—March, 1964. A tidal wave generated by the Alaska earthquake destroyed 29 square blocks of the city, killed 12, and injured countless others. Police were involved in emergency evacuation, prevention of re-entry, and looting.

Richmond, Indiana—Feb., 1965. A fire destroyed telephone communications for the entire area for three days. Police were required to provide extra security patrols for all banking and financial institutions, and provide emergency citizens band radio communications stations throughout the community so that citizens could report fires or request police assistance.

Carson, Calif.—July, 1969. An explosion at an industrial plant released a low-hanging cloud of poisonous gas. Police were required to immediately evacuate over two thousand residents downwind of the location, prevent re-entry, control panic, and provide emergency hospital transportation for those persons overcome by the fumes.

San Fernando, Calif.—Feb., 1971. A major earthquake destroyed telephone communications, water, and gas, collapsed freeway overpasses and bridges, and created extreme destruction. Police were involved in instituting extra security patrols to prevent looting, searches in debris for dead and injured, and establishing temporary emergency communications service.

Do each of the above described incidents meet the author's definition of disaster? Note that in some there were no deaths, in others there was no identifiable property damage.

PURPOSE OF THIS BOOK

It was the author's purpose to provide the reader with a frame of reference for disaster planning, be he a police administrator or a student in a police science classroom. The basic principles underlying disaster management are presented in such a way that those applicable may be modified to fit varying circumstances and different sized police agencies. The subject of command post management is dealt with in some depth as well as is the topic of evacuation. Although usually handled by the fire, medical, or coroners departments, the topics of rescue from debris, casualty sorting, and body recovery are included.

In another section of this book the reader will find a discussion of the basic incidents which are considered disasters. A number of case studies of police disaster operations are presented as well as the psychological problems which occur during disaster. A special section concerns the topic of panic control.

2
DISASTER ROLE OF THE POLICE

Because of the rather low esteem with which it is held in this country, the author hestitates to mention the term, "Civil Defense." Yet police disaster control is historically and necessarily linked with the community's civil defense structure. It is unfortunate that during the past twenty-five years the concept of civil defense has been so strongly linked with protection against enemy attack and nuclear survival. The fact that these incidents have not happened, coupled with a strong public opinion that should they happen civil defense would be of no avail, has caused the civil defense concept to become a stepchild. Given little attention by the legislative process, virtually ignored in the area of funds and staffing, continually renamed and reassigned to various branches of government by our executive branch, it is little wonder that the public in general and public safety employees in particular resist identifying with the civil defense concept.

Perhaps had the civil defense concept been grounded in routine community disaster control from the onset, it would have achieved far wider acceptance. Had it been structured to meet floods, earthquakes, tornadoes, hurricanes, and other catastrophes instead of nuclear disaster, it might have proven its true need and effectiveness. This has, of course, not been the case.

RESPONSIBILITY OF LOCAL GOVERNMENT

In briefly describing the disaster responsibilities of local government it becomes necessary to also identify the role of the Federal and state governments.

Federal Civil Defense

Our Federal Civil Defense Agency is primarily a staff or service organization. Although it coordinates a national warning system its primary functions of interest to local law enforcement agencies are research, training, and supply.

The primary emphasis of civil defense research in the past has been nuclear survival. Projects have included study of the ability of various types of structures to withstand blasts, extensive study of radiation and radiation dangers, experimentation with food storage, food and water purification, emergency and mass sanitation problems. While the basic assumption behind this research was nuclear survival, many of the by-products have been of value in normal disaster control. In addition, most of the emergency control procedures for civilian nuclear energy accidents have resulted from this research.

Based on the results of their research, the Federal Civil Defense Agency has created an extensive training program. Most of this training has grown within the structure of nuclear survival, but portions of the material developed are of value in local disaster control; for example, search and removal from debris, panic control, emergency casualty sorting and handling. A wide range of training bulletins, course outlines, training films, pamphlets, and other materials are made available by the Federal Civil Defense Agency, many of which are of value to local police training officers.

The third important staff function of the Federal Civil Defense Agency is testing, recommendation, and provision of materials or supplies to local governments. Some of these materials are surplus, others are recommended for purchase and partially funded through a dollar matching agreement between Federal and local governments. Through such arrangements many local law enforcement agencies have obtained a variety of radio, telephone, and other communications equipment, vehicles, emergency lighting equipment, and other materials which are of extreme value during local emergencies.

In addition to their warning, research, training and supply functions, the Federal Civil Defense Agency provides suggested organizational structures for state and local governments and supplements these suggestions with staff planning assistance.

State Civil Defense

Virtually every state has a civil defense organization. They may be difficult to recognize immediately by title, for example, State Disaster Office, Emergency Planning Commission, or Bureau of Emergency Operations. For the most part, the state agencies operate in much the same role as the federal agency by providing some research, training, and supply services.

In recent years, these state agencies have acquired a new role, that of coordinating mutual aid between the various political subdivisions of the state during an emergency. For example, the California State Disaster Office has divided the state into a number of regions. Each region has a Regional Coordinator and is further divided into areas which are coordinated by an Area Coordinator. Much of the efforts of the California State Disaster Office are directed toward insuring that maximum resources are utilized at the local level, through mutual aid, before other areas within a region are requested to provide assistance. This system assures that full local and regional resources are committed prior to requests for activation of the National Guard or federal assistance. (See Appendix A—Chap. 8.)

In addition, many state civil defense agencies provide a reservoir of emergency equipment for use throughout the state as needed. This may consist of a number of fire trucks, field hospitals, portable command posts or communication centers, portable chemical toilets, and field kitchens. The theory being that since no individual local community can afford such emergency equipment, when a disaster occurs, such equipment may be immediately loaned by the state to the county or city in need. One advantage to this theory is that should a city buy a local field kitchen, it might use it only once in ten years; but when the state acquires such a unit, it may be used on a state-wide basis as frequently as once a year.

Local Civil Defense

The theory of civil defense in the United States is based on local government providing basic services. Thus each local government (city or county) usually has a civil defense plan and has established a civil defense organization. These plans provide for the creation of a number of civil defense services which operate under a director.

Although their number vary, some civil defense organizations have as many as fourteen services. Following federal planning guidelines, these services may be designated as: fire, police, evacuation, communications, supply, engineering, warden, utilities, etc. Each of the services that compose the local civil defense organization are made up of the most logical normal functioning counterpart. For example, the fire service under civilian defense organization is actually the community's fire department.

Where there is not a city department to function as a civil defense service, a private organization or community association may be substituted. For example, where a community does not have a public water or power utility, a private utility company providing this resource becomes the "utility service." Thus the American Red Cross, the Salvation Army, the Boy Scouts, and a variety of other organizations will find themselves described in a local community's civil defense organizational chart.

The theory of local response is that when the emergency or a given set of declarations occur, the normal organizational structure of community government dissolves. New laws go into effect for the period of the emergency, and the streamlined and efficient civil defense organization commanded by a director, takes over the government of the community until conditions have been normalized. Under this streamlined civil defense organization new levels of authority and areas of responsibility may be delegated to existing personnel and agencies. For example, under normal circumstances, the police chief and fire chief might rank equally and neither could give the other orders or command performance. Additionally, during normal conditions a municipal employee disobeying an order might be subject to termination or other discipline. Under emergency conditions, when the local civil defense organization is in operation, the police chief might be filling the role of the "Director of Civil Defense" and might then be able to give orders to the fire chief, the city engineer, the city clerk, the local Red Cross director and the city health officer. Under the city's Emergency Civil Defense Ordinance, failure to obey these orders might constitute a public offense and subject the offender to a fine or imprisonment.

Activation of Local Civil Defense

The civil defense organization cannot replace local government on a mere whim or due to unfounded or unverified emergencies. The activation of local civil defense is almost universally governed by law and requires a number of circumstances to occur. For example, in one state the civil defense apparatus can be activated only if the governor has made an appropriate declaration of "disaster" or "extreme emergency," or if the chief executive of a city or county has declared a "state of local peril." In some jurisdictions, local declarations can be made only upon the approval of the City Council or the County Board of Supervisors. In a few states, the governor's declaration is dependent upon ratification by state legislative body or by an emergency planning council.

When such a declaration has been made, however, the civil defense organization replaces the normal community governmental structure; and while all other laws remain in effect, the community or states disaster law or civil defense ordinance becomes operative. These laws and ordinances provide for the declaration of a curfew, the seizure of private property for public use, penalties for failure to respond to lawful orders of those granted command authority under the new civil defense organization, and a variety of other regulations which Americans would not countenance under normal conditions.

It is obvious that the seriousness of such changes in authority and responsibility require activation of the civil defense organization only upon some type of legal proclamation or process. It is also obvious that the time consumed in obtaining such a proclamation, coupled with the fact that little may occur until the proclamation has been confirmed, is one element which can cause community response to a disaster to be slow, cumbersome, and inefficient.

The Police Service

As mentioned previously, one branch of civil defense organization is the "police service." This is the police department in cities, or the sheriff's department in the counties. After the proper declarations have been made, the police service functions under the Director of Civil Defense for the duration of the emergency. Guidelines provided by the Federal Civil Defense Agency indicate that the following are the primary responsibilities of the police service.

1. Evacuation.
2. Post attack recovery techniques.
3. Control of civilian and military traffic.
4. Control of ingress and egress from contaminated areas.
5. Security and protection of vital facilities.
6. Enforcement of special economic stabilization measures.
7. Explosive ordinance reconnaissance.

It is obvious that the Federal Civil Defense Agency has been preoccupied with the threat of nuclear attack and it is unfortunate that most of the planning and training to date, among most police departments, has been directed toward the previously listed guidelines. These guidelines and related training do not frequently relate to the demands made upon police agencies during the more common disasters.

THE PROBLEM OF POLICE RESPONSE

Pre-Proclamation

Police departments respond and attempt to control disasters, in cooperation with various other emergency public service agencies, from the moment of occurrence until the proclamation establishes them as a subordinate service under the civil defense organization. This interim period may range from as little as two hours to as long as several days. During this interim period, the police department may be in full control of the response.

It has been proven in many instances that how well and how rapidly the police department responds during the first fifteen minutes to two hours of a disaster can make a tremendous difference in the number of casualties and the amount of property damage suffered. The nature of their response can also make a marked difference in the success or failure of the community civil defense organization, once it has been activated. It must be stressed that during this interim period, the response of the police department is solely their responsibility and is usually under no control or direction by the civil defense organization.

No Proclamation

In many cases police response (combined with other public safety agencies) is so prompt and effective that the threat of the disaster or emergency is rapidly neutralized, thus making it unnecessary for local authorities or the governor to make a declaration. Thus, during many disasters of low profile, the community's civil defense organization is never activated and the community's response is made solely by the police and other public safety agencies.

POLICE DISASTER ACTIVITIES

From the foregoing, it can be seen that the police face a dichotomy so far as their concern with the civil defense organization is concerned. On the one hand, they must respond and operate well in advance of, and in many cases without, the community's civil defense organization being activated. On the other hand, they must constantly be cognizant of the community's civil defense organization because: a) how they perform in the interim may markedly affect the efficiency of the total civil defense effort when a proclamation is made, b) if a proclamation is issued and the civil defense organization becomes operative, the police must function under its authority and coordinate effectively with the other services. In any event, it is appropriate here to list the police functions which are involved in their disaster control role, recognizing that the making of any list may involve unintended omissions.

Primary Police Role

The following are considered to be the most important functions of the police during a disaster. Their numerical listing does not indicate priority.

1. Protect life and property generally.
2. Provide first-aid to victims.
3. Evacuate population groups where necessary.
4. Search for and rescue the injured.
5. Cordon the area to prevent entry.
6. Establish traffic corridors and control.
7. Prevent looting.
8. Notify all agencies or organizations involved.
9. Panic control at the scene.
10. Crowd control on the perimeter.
11. Casualty sorting at the scene.
12. Establishing or maintaining the mutual aid plan.
13. Maintaining a level of police service in area outside disaster.
14. Organize and direct activities of volunteers.
15. Determine total or exact nature and scope of disaster.

Secondary Police Role

The following functions, although important, are generally considered to be of such a nature that in most instances they should be given secondary priority.

1. Recover and protect the dead.
2. Maintain chronological record of incident (log).
3. Complete damage reports.
4. Recover and safeguard property.
5. Identify the dead.
6. Notify surviving kin of dead and injured.
7. Issue and control passes into control area.
8. Photograph, document, and record damage.
9. Facilitate accurate news coverage.
10. Take missing persons reports.

SUMMARY

Local law enforcement agencies are traditionally organized as a service of the community's civil defense for emergency disaster response. Unfortunately civil defense emphasis has been primarily in the area of war related or nuclear incidents. Such training or techniques are of little use in most disasters.

The police must respond to disaster control well in advance of community civil defense response, yet become a part of it later. For these reasons the police disaster response must be developed outside the authority of the civil defense organization, yet be designed to mesh with it during the latter phases of the incident.

3
POLICE DISASTER PLANNING

Keeping in mind the unique role of the police in disaster response with respect to civil defense relationships, it follows that at least two plans should be developed: one for the interim period, where the police operate independently, and one for the latter stages of disaster control, where the police must operate as a subordinate part of the total community response.

ORGANIZATION AND FUNCTION PLAN

A comprehensive plan must be designed to guide police management through the primary and terminal periods of their disaster operations. Such plans are usually of little use during the initial police response to disaster; however, they become vitally important when large numbers of personnel have been massed, when the administrative hierarchy has responded, and when the law enforcement agency must cooperate and coordinate its operations with other organizations or must operate under the authority of the civil defense structure. This type of plan is often required under mutual aid agreements with other communities (see Appendix B). Such plans may also be required by civil defense authorities of each civil defense "service" in order to insure the elimination of overlap and conflict.

Organization and function plans vary widely as to content, format, and detail. Experience has shown that such plans should be detailed enough to provide guidelines for action yet should be general enough to permit individual initiative on the part of those who must put the plan into action. Experience has also shown that plans which are designed to be utilized in specific types of disaster are usually of much less value than an overall disaster plan, as management and administration problems tend to differ little from one type of emergency situation to another.

Policy Statements

The organization and function plan should contain a number of statements which provide guidelines for action and acceptable limits of deviation. These statements must be sufficiently simple and clear to provide the police administrator with a frame of reference for decision making under stress. Such policy statements should include guidelines for establishing a separate command over the disaster and the maintaining of a given level of police service in the surrounding unaffected community under another command. Guidelines should also be provided to administrators on the utilization of manpower with respect to their authority to order overtime, requirements for release of on-duty officers, and the assignment or release of mutual aid personnel from adjoining communities. Policy statements should include operational techniques where experience or legal advice indicates that it is appropriate, for example:

> In the event of an ordered dispersal from a disaster area by either a higher authority or the law enforcement commander on the scene, law enforcement personnel from this city will assist and direct the movement of the flow of traffic to the limits of this jurisdiction only.

Experience has shown that the management of many disaster control activities can be endangered by conflict in command. Clear-cut policy statements should be included in the organization and function plan to clarify the authority and the assignment of command. Statements such as the following may seem superfluous, but have proven highly important in past incidents:

> The field commander, regardless of rank, shall have complete authority and responsibility for conducting the field operations during an unusual occurrence or disaster.

Other statements are required to clarify the role of subordinate managers and supervisors, for example:

> All personnel within, assisting or assigned to the involved area shall be subject to the direct command and supervision of the field commander. Supervisors of employees assigned to the involved area as specialists shall exercise functional but not line supervision over such employees.

During the primary and terminal stages of the disaster many high-ranking police authorities, community leaders, and persons whose presence may be politically necessary usually appear in and around the affected area. Some organization and function plans have found necessary a policy statement to clarify the role of these dignitaries:

> The mere presence of a ranking senior officer at the scene of an unusual occurrence or disaster shall not indicate his assumption of command. Such ranking senior officer shall remain in an advisory and/or evaluating capacity unless he specifically assumes command.

Legal Clarification

The organization and function plan must provide an explanation of the legal authority and responsibility of police officials who must administer the plan. An explanation of, and appropriate excerpts from, the city's civil defense or disaster ordinance should be included. Various proclamations which might be made by the President of the United States, the Governor of the concerned state, or the Mayor or other authorized community leader in the local jurisdiction should be carefully explained. Clarifications of the legality of the administrator's involvement in mutual aid, evacuation, and other problems should be included, particularly where he may incur some civil liability through his actions.

Definitions

The organization and function plan necessarily takes the police administrator into new experiences. Since both he and subordinates, as well as members of other organizations, may be utilizing the organization and function plan, it is important that all have the same understanding regarding terms used. The plan should be examined and when a term is found that is unusual or which may have a different meaning to various persons concerned, that term should be defined. Typical examples of such terms are as follows:

1. *Day-to-day mutual aid* means aid performed in accordance with the Mutual Aid Agreements on a voluntary basis.

2. *Emergency mutual aid* means mutual aid rendered after a "state of disaster" or a "state of extreme emergency" has been declared by the governor.
3. *State law enforcement coordinator* means that person appointed by the governor to serve in such capacity.
4. *Regional law enforcement coordinator* means the person selected to act in such capacity in any region of the state by the operational law enforcement coordinator of such region.
5. *Operational area law enforcement coordinator* means the person selected to act in such capacity in any operational area in accordance with procedures established in such area.
6. *Mutual aid region* means any area of the state designated by the governor in accordance with the authority contained in the California Disaster Act.
7. *Unusual occurrence* means an unscheduled physical event involving actual or potential personal injury or property damage arising from fire, flood, storm, earthquake, land slide, wreck, or other natural or man-caused incident requiring police action, but in the control of which the police are not the primary agent.
8. *Area.* A physical location at which the unusual occurrence exists.
9. *Closed area.* An area where ingress or egress to vehicular or pedestrian traffic is restricted on three or more sides.

The number of terms requiring definition in an organization and function plan is usually related to the complexity of the plan, the size of the agency for whom the plan has been prepared, and the sophistication or level of training of departmental command personnel.

Order of Succession

The question of who shall command during disaster frequently occurs. Obviously the chief of police or the sheriff commands the organization. But in his absence, or until he officially designates a commander for the incident, who shall command? In many disasters law enforcement officials have assumed command in an authority vacuum where no one in the department was quite sure who should actually have the authority or responsibility.

One important portion of the organization and function plan is the establishment of who, under what conditions and circumstances, shall command. In many plans, this is merely a progressive statement such as, "In the absence of the chief of police, the captain of the patrol division shall command; and in his absence, the captain of the detective division shall command; and in his absence, the captain of the services division shall command; and in his absence, the lieutenant then on duty in the patrol bureau shall command, etc."

Departments which have utilized a plan such as this through several disasters usually amend it in such a way that actual rank is not designated. In most disasters, the person logically best equipped to command is that administrator in the patrol or field operations unit who has been most involved with the incident since its occurrence. His rank may vary from sergeant through deputy chief. During normal operations, it will be found that some officer will be in charge of every police operation: patrol watch, detective unit, jail, or traffic enforcement unit. His function in a disaster is determined primarily by the services, manpower, and equipment his unit can provide, not his rank. It therefore simplifies matters considerably to have an order of succession statement which states that in the absence of the chief, the commander of the patrol division shall assume command, etc. In this case, the commander of the patrol division may be a lieutenant during evening hours, perhaps a captain in the daytime, conceivably even a sergeant during a summer vacation period or in the early hours of the morning.

Duties of Personnel

The organization and function plan must contain a number of duty statements or position descriptions to clarify the role of administrators, managers, supervisors, and specialist police personnel who are charged with new or different responsibilities during the disaster, or whose disaster related objectives are new, unusual, or little related to normal police functions. Such duty statements are usually of two types: a) general statements for administrators and supervisors to clarify their new roles and relationships, and b) job descriptions for staff officers who are executing a new or unusual role. An example of the first type of duty statement might be as follows:

> The chief of police of the city of _____ will be in complete charge of all law enforcement personnel operating within the city. This will include regulars, auxiliaries, and any other law enforcement personnel from other jurisdictions that may report for duty within this jurisdiction. He will select and assign to the city control center an officer to act as the liaison officer between his office and the control center. He shall establish and maintain liaison with the operational area law enforcement coordinator, and through him with the regional law enforcement coordinator in order to relate local plans to state plans for law enforcement civil defense services.

Examples of the second type of duty statement, relating specifically to command post functions, might be as follows:

1. *Executive Officer—Functions:* Under the direction of the emergency control center commander, the executive officer shall exercise line supervision over the assigned personnel and the functional operation of the emergency control center. He shall be acting commander of the emergency control center during the absence of the commander.
2. *Intelligence Officer—Functions:* The intelligence officer shall be responsible for coordination of the activities of the intelligence section and shall exercise supervision over the personnel assigned to the section.
3. *Journal Clerk—Functions:* The journal clerk shall be responsible for preparation and maintenance of the emergency control center journal and performance of other clerical tasks, as required.
4. *Map Officer—Functions:* The map officer shall be responsible for posting all maps in the emergency control center, communications division, and public service section with pertinent information.

5. *Situation Report Officer—Functions:* The situation report officer is reponsible for gathering such information as will enable him to have a total cognizance of the unusual occurrence. He shall be prepared to brief authorized personnel, civic officers, and other important persons on pertinent matters relative to the unusual occurrence.

Note that in the above statements no rank is implied for the individual as these are position duty statements and might conceivably be filled by officers of any line or staff rank.

Changes in Unit Functions

Under a normal organization plan for a police department, each subdivision or unit of the department has clearly defined duties, functions, and responsibilities. During disaster control operations, however, these duties, functions, and responsibilities may be greatly altered or a given unit may have one primary responsibility at the time of occurrence of the disaster, another primary responsibility during the period of overall disaster operations, and still a third unusual responsibility in the post-disaster period.

For example, at the time of occurrence of a disaster a detective bureau, whose primary function is the investigation of crime and prosecution of offenders, may suddenly find that its primary role is providing manpower to the patrol division to enable that unit to achieve early control. Some hours or even days after the occurrence of the disaster, and during the police department's disaster control operations, the detective bureau may find that the majority of its personnel are assigned to evacuation centers to participate in the registration of evacuees, or in operations to assist the coroner, such as the identification of the dead, or conducting missing persons investigations. In the weeks following the disaster, the detective bureau may be considerably utilized in the identification, registration, and return of recovered property to disaster victims.

The organization and function plan must contain some policy which will guide the chief and the unit commanders in shifting the emphasis of their unit's operation from phase to phase of the disaster, and in allocating available manpower from unit to unit.

Such general advance planning for changes in function or responsibility and for balancing of manpower tend to insure cooperation and efficiency during the disaster. Planning of this kind not done until the disaster occurs results in operational chaos, open clashes between unit administrators, and the creation of long-term bad feelings or jealousies among the command hierarchy (see Appendix C and D, Chap. 8).

Testing and Training

Once an organization and function plan has been developed for a department, its effectiveness can be determined only by use during a disaster. However, the ability of personnel to function with the plan, and omissions or errors in planning may be detected by a combination of testing and training called "simulation." Command post type disaster simulations should be held, probably no less than six months apart, wherein the administrative and mid-management levels of the department are involved in exercises which require them to place the organization and function plan into operation. Such exercises are most effective when carried out in cooperation with other community disaster services.

In California operation "cable-splicer" is carried out annually and permits law enforcement authorities in every jurisdiction to participate in a mutual exercise involving coordination with the National Guard, state disaster office, regional and area coordinators. While such simulations are generally of the "in-basket—out-basket" type some agencies have managed to inject extensive realism through role playing (see Appendix E, Chap. 8).

EMERGENCY RESPONSE PLAN

The emergency response plan differs from the organization and function plan in that the response plan is designed to be used by the on-duty commander and his personnel from the time a "non-warning" disaster occurs until such time as the more formalized organization and function plan can go into operation. The emergency response plan must be simple, flexible, and above all, it must be available. The plan, or portions thereof, must be in the hands of line personnel. As with the organization and function plan, the emergency response plan must provide guidelines to action which permit and encourage initiative on the part of the executing officers. In addition, the emergency response plan should provide the on-duty commander with a number of self-executing systems which simplify delegation of responsibility during this period of extreme stress and confusion.

The importance of effective police disaster operations during the first period of the incident (from the time of occurrence until the second or third hour) cannot be overstated. The procedures and operations that the on-duty commander initiates during this period often affect total control time, total injuries, deaths, and property damage sustained during the disaster. For example, an evacuation of five hundred residents from a given area may consume one hour and thirty minutes from the time the first patrol car enters the area until the last house is inspected and the cordon established. Such an evacuation may require the assignment of twenty-five policemen. How soon the police commander institutes a manpower call-up or a mutual aid request to obtain the extra officers required for the evacuation operation, and how soon he determines such an operation is necessary and orders it executed, obviously determines the time at which the residents will be able to be cleared from the area. If an approaching forest fire, structural fire, or high water from a broken dam is moving toward the affected area at a predicted speed, and if the disaster commander has failed at an earlier stage to institute a proper manpower build-up, the cost in deaths, injuries, and property loss in the area will necessarily be greater.

At a later time during the disaster, because of this failure during the initial stage, a portion of the manpower available must be detailed to the recovery and identification of property in the affected area which might have otherwise been safely removed. In addition, police personnel may be assigned to missing persons and body recovery or identification functions, whereas an evacuation might have made this unnecessary. In one incident after another, it has been documented that police operations during the first few hours of a disaster can materially affect the overall handling of the entire incident.

Format

The key to a successful emergency response plan is simplicity and flexibility. Therefore, the plan must not be so long that it becomes self-defeating. It must be general enough to apply to all situations which may occur, must encourage individual initiative, and must be constantly available to all line officers who may have to put it into operation.

Two basic types of format have generally evolved which meet these criteria. The first is a three to four page plan which briefly states the duties and responsibilities of different units or members of the department who may be on duty when an unusual occurrence or disaster occurs. Such a plan is usually kept posted on patrol bulletin boards, reproduced as roll call training and included in watch commander's, unit commander's, and supervisor's notebooks. (See Appendix F, Chap. 8.)

In the second type of format, individual functions and duty statements are briefly described and printed on billfold sized cards. These cards are then issued to personnel and carried with them at all times. For example, one type of card would be printed, sealed in plastic, and issued to patrolmen; another type would be issued to on-duty detectives; and another type to civilian records or communications personnel. Probably a combination of the two formats would be most effective: a basic, simple, flexible plan, available as previously described, supplemented by personnel duty statement cards issued to all concerned personnel.

Duty Statements

Short statements as to the duties of line personnel during the early stages of a disaster are necessarily included in the disaster response plan. Such statements as the following are common:

First Officer on the Scene

1. Determine and communicate to headquarters the type and location of the disaster or unusual occurrence.
2. Render emergency medical assistance.
3. Organize volunteer self-help at the scene.

4. Assume interim command at the scene and direct the activities of second and subsequent officers to arrive.
5. Stay available for radio communications at all times.
6. Start a chronological listing of events in the notebook.
7. Relinquish command and give a situational briefing to the first supervisor to arrive.

Second Officer on the Scene

The second officer at the scene of a disaster shall perform the following duties:
1. Under the direction of the first officer on the scene, determine and communicate to headquarters the range of the unusual occurrence.
2. Determine and communicate the exact type and location of the following hazards:
    a. power lines down.
    b. broken water mains.
    c. escaping vapors.
    d. blocked streets.
    e. fires.
    f. cave-ins.
    g. land slides.
    h. structural damage.
    i. crowd or panic conditions.
    j. traffic congestion.

First Supervisor on the Scene

The first supervisor on the scene of the disaster shall perform the following:
1. Assume interim command.
2. Assume and inspect all duties executed by first officer at the scene.
3. Establish a command post.
4. Advise headquarters of probable manpower requirements, need to cordon area, traffic control problems, and equipment or materials needed.

The number of such statements and their detail depend on the size of the police department concerned and its degree of specialization, but at a minimum such instruction should be included for field officers, supervisors, unit or watch commanders, and station or communications personnel.

SELF-EXECUTING SYSTEMS

An invaluable portion of each emergency response plan is a series of self-executing systems. These systems are pre-planned, designed, and packaged so that they may be put into operation by a unit commander in time of stress with as little confusion as possible. They are specifically designed to give the commander a concise statement of his authority and responsibility with respect to the particular problem the system is designed to meet, and in addition, the system is so assembled that it may be immediately delegated to someone of lesser rank for execution.

Ideally each system is contained in a manila envelope in the watch commander's desk drawer, plainly and clearly marked. All he need do is open the drawer, withdraw the proper envelope, open it, or read on its cover the short statement regarding his authority and responsibility with respect to the problem, hand the envelope to a subordinate and order him to execute its contents. The unit commander should not again be bothered with detail regarding the system. Detailed examples of several self-executing systems which should be included in the disaster response plan must be discussed.

Manpower Recall System

Although the most immediate source of manpower for assistance during a disaster is usually mutual aid, a recall of departmental off-duty manpower, reserves and others, must be implemented early in the disaster control operation so that mutual aid forces may be released and adequate manpower will be available during the later control phases of the disaster. When it is determined that a manpower recall is necessary, the unit commander should select the envelope containing this system, and from its cover quickly review his department's policy on authority to recall off-duty personnel and reserves. Such a statement should permit any commander to determine if the situation gives him the authority to execute the system. If he determines that he has such authority, the package should be opened.

The first item in the package should be a departmental policy statement as to who is to be recalled, and in what order. For example, should those officers who will next go on regular duty be called in first? Has provision been made to hold over officers now on duty, or should any personnel that can be contacted be ordered to duty?

The method of call-up then must be selected by the unit commander. Usually, two are provided, fan-out and direct. Under a fan-out system, each member of the department has a complete list of the addresses and the telephone numbers of all other personnel. The fan-out procedure is usually most effective in small and medium-sized police agencies. Under the fan-out system the person delegated to execute the call-up system contacts only one, two or perhaps three off-duty personnel. He advises each officer of the call-up and advises them to continue the call-up from their home telephones. This type of system takes a great load off the police telephone system at the station and permits on-duty station personnel to be concerned with other important tasks. The direct system involves calling directly each off-duty officer from the police station.

The unit commander will then find in the system a message form which he must complete. An exact message must be given to each member of the department who is being recalled. This message must advise him where to report, what equipment to bring with him or uniform to wear, and approximately how long he can be expected to be on duty.

The unit commander, having opened the package, determined what order of call-up to use, determined the system of call-up to use, and determined the message to be given to those called up, hands the system to a subordinate to execute. The system package contains the names, telephone numbers, alternate telephone numbers, addresses and other data, needed for recall.

An effective manpower recall system depends on much more than the contents and organization of this package, however. Departmental policy and training must make it clear to all exactly what their actions should be upon receiving an order to respond to duty, or on what they must do if they become aware of a disaster or unusual occurrence while in an off-duty status and prior to receiving an official recall communication. These policies and procedures are a matter of individual discretion for various police departments depending upon their size and geographic area. Some departments prefer not to have off-duty personnel calling the station during a disaster to inquire if their services are needed. Other departments make it mandatory that an off-duty officer, upon learning of a disaster or unusual occurrence in progress, immediately report to the station or other designated locations.

Some police departments have developed a recall alert code which can be broadcast by radio and television stations. The recall code must be one which will be heard or understood by all personnel yet which will not incite community panic or reveal the nature and location of the incident. For example, all officers might be trained to respond to the police department upon hearing "attention all Glenville public safety employees—a signal fifteen is now in effect." The advantages of such an alert system must be weighed against its disadvantages. While it may quickly contact the significant number of off-duty officers (depending upon the time of day), it may also trigger a number of telephone calls to the police station from curious citizens inquiring as to the nature of the situation. If such a system is adopted, previous arrangements must be made with the broadcasting media, and some code identification system must be established and included in the manpower call-up system so that pranksters could not call up radio stations impersonating police officials and simulate false manpower call-ups as a hoax.

The manpower call-up system must also make provision for a survey of the police station periodically for off-duty personnel who may be in the station but are unaware that a disaster has occurred or that a call-up is in progress. It has occurred in situations where the nature of the disaster was somewhat concealed and where the police station was a large and rambling building, that off-duty personnel were utilizing the department basement pistol range, were coming into and out of the locker room from the parking lot with clean uniforms for their lockers, or for other purposes, and were picking up their paychecks from the city clerk at the same time a police desk officer was attempting to locate them at home for a recall to duty. Some manpower recall systems provide that every fifteen minutes the public address system or intercommunication unit within the department should carry a message to all stations describing the nature of the alert. Other systems require a designated officer to make a periodic tour of the station to attempt to locate any personnel who may not be aware of the nature of the emergency.

The effectiveness of any manpower recall plan is dependent upon two elements: a) the effectiveness of the recall system, and b) the amount of "role conflict" that is experienced by the officer during the disaster. The police officer has many roles! He is a dedicated professional peace officer, he is a father, a husband, a property owner, and occasionally a very frightened individual. Given a disaster of sufficient magnitude, the off-duty policeman may select the primary role of survival, or the primary role of protection of family or property in preference to the role of responding police officer. Policemen are more likely to respond to their official role during disaster if they are members of a department where the morale is high or they are certain that their services will be well and productively used, and where they are convinced that their response in police assignment will be to the maximum benefit of their family as well as the community in general.

Some police departments have conducted family and individual survival training sessions in cooperation with various civil defense organizations. All departmental personnel and their families attend this training and in addition to receiving valuable instruction are assisted in equipping their homes for maximum survival. These agencies are convinced that an officer who feels that his family is safe will respond to duty much more quickly than one who does not. They feel that an investment in family training and survival will have payoffs in manpower recall when needed.

No manpower recall system should be accepted without testing and experimentation. Initial and periodic practice drills should be held and the percentage of officers contacted by various elements of the system should carefully be recorded for later analysis. Officers contacted on some occasions should merely be required to state their degree of readiness to respond and estimate their time of arrival at the station. Occasionally, however, actual physical recalls should be made so that unit commanders will have an accurate estimate of the amount of time that it takes given percentages of officers, at given times of day, to respond to the station. Only equipped with such estimates can they effectively plan to utilize manpower recalled on an emergency basis during a disaster.

Notification System

When disaster strikes, the police department is responsible for making a number of notifications. In some cases, these notifications are directly related to effective disaster control operations. In other instances, notifications have little to do with actual operational effectiveness, but are more concerned with achieving and maintaining political harmony and favorable public relations. To avoid duplication and to eliminate later recriminations, there must be some verification of notification. Some agencies list all notifications completed on a disaster log. This can occasionally be cumbersome, and invites omissions.

A good notification system provides the identity of the persons notified, the message transmitted, and verification of notification all within the system. Here, again, a manila envelope in the unit commander's drawer labeled "notification system," permits him to delegate this task to a subordinate and insures accurate completion of the task.

Inside the master envelope are a number of smaller envelopes and a message form. The watch commander completes the message form. This is the statement that will be transmitted to those persons to be notified. Each envelope contains the name, telephone number, address, or other data on persons or agencies of a given class to be notified. For example, in the press notification envelope could be information relative to a central press number or each newspaper, radio station and television station in the community. In the utilities envelope, might be the gas, water, power and telephone company emergency telephone numbers and other data. A hospital notification envelope would include the emergency number of the admitting desk of each hospital within the area. A community notification envelope would contain notification data for all city, county, and state agencies plus those political notifications which must be made.

With such a system, the unit commander needs only to open the master envelope, write the message, determine the priority of notification, perhaps eliminating some notifications if appropriate, and hand the system to a subordinate to execute. The subordinate calls the person or agency indicated and on the prepared form notes the time and the name of the person to whom he gave the message. Such a system eliminates the omission of an important notification, permits priority to be given to the notifications, verifies each notification for later documentary purposes, does not burden the log officer with needless entries, and requires no further supervision on the part of the unit commander.

Mutual Aid Systems

When disaster strikes and the unit commander needs additional manpower on an emergency basis, it is usually more readily available from those policemen who are on-duty in surrounding or neighboring communities than from recalling off-duty departmental personnel. Highway patrolmen, deputy sheriffs, and policemen from the surrounding jurisdictions can usually arrive and be effectively deployed at a disaster from twenty to thirty minutes more quickly than can the agencies off-duty and reserve officers who are recalled. Mutual aid systems exist under a variety of arrangements throughout the United States. Some are informal, others are formalized agreements, while still others are in the nature of a formal contract.

When a unit commander requests mutual aid in an emergency or when he is requested to provide mutual aid to a neighboring agency, the task is greatly simplified if he can again reach into his desk drawer and withdraw a manila envelope labeled "mutual aid systems." On the face of the envelope is his department's policy on the authority to request mutual aid or to grant mutual aid to other agencies, and under what circumstances. From the face of the envelope, the unit commander can quickly determine if the situation calls for his further involvement in the mutual aid system. If it does, he opens the envelope, and removes the request form. This form requires him to enter the nature of the emergency, the agency to be contacted for help, the location where reporting mutual aid officers should respond, the equipment that they should bring with them, and whether he requests supervisors in addition to policemen. This form may be immediately handed to a subordinate who will place the requests. Attached to the form are the names and telephone numbers of those agencies authorized to provide mutual aid and a verification system upon which the subordinate can record the time and person contacted regarding the request.

Also in the mutual aid system envelope will be some policy statements and guidelines with respect to the type of assignment to be given to responding mutual aid personnel. The unit commander may transmit this information to his supervisors on the scene of the disaster, issue it to his "personnel officer" or retain it for future consideration. It has been found in the past that policemen responding into another jurisdiction under mutual aid are best used for traffic control, cordoning, crowd control, and other operations on the perimeter of the disaster. Mutual aid agreements are usually most harmonious where responding officers are not injured and responding equipment is not damaged. It is the underlying philosophy of mutual aid that the law enforcement agency having jurisdiction of the disaster should be the agency to suffer the maximum personnel injury, expense or equipment damage. Therefore, responding personnel should usually be assigned to support positions or the policing of the community and not committed to actual hazardous disaster control functions.

In addition, the mutual aid system envelope should contain a departmental policy on continued survey of the disaster scene and release of mutual aid forces. It should be understood that the neighboring police department which has provided manpower and equipment is probably operating their community at a reduced level of efficiency. They fully expect to have their personnel and equipment returned to them as soon as it is no longer required at the scene of the disaster. For this reason it becomes incumbent upon the requesting agency to continually survey the disaster area and release those mutual aid forces that are no longer needed.

A separate envelope in the mutual aid system package contains information for the unit commander who may be required to provide mutual aid to a neighboring agency. Information in this envelope should provide him with guidelines on how many personnel to send, how to select them, what equipment to provide, and whether or not to send a supervisor. Over the years, experience with mutual aid has shown that it is most effective when the responding agency sends its own supervisors with patrolmen. Patrolmen are more easily controlled and more responsive when supervised by the sergeants to whom they must regularly answer, than when supervised by the staff of a neighboring agency.

Evacuation System

Many disasters require the disaster commander to place an evacuation plan into operation. Threatening fire, flood, or toxic fumes may require large numbers of citizens to be removed from areas of residence or employment for several hours, and occasionally for days or weeks. The need to execute an evacuation plan usually occurs while a commander is fully preoccupied with the stress of the entire disaster control operation. The task is made more expedient if he has a prepackaged evacuation system.

Again the commander retrieves a large manila envelope which has on its cover a statement of his legal authority to order an evacuation and departmental policy on his execution of this authority. For example, in California, this would be a statement of Penal Code Section 409.5:

Whenever a menace to the public health or safety is created by a calamity such as flood, storm, fire, earthquake, explosion, accident, or other disaster, officers of the California Highway Patrol, police departments, or sheriff's office may close thereof by means of ropes, markers, or guards to any and all persons not authorized by such officer to enter or remain within the closed area. Any person not authorized willfully entering the area or willfully remaining within the area after notice to evacuate shall be guilty of a misdemeanor.

Nothing in this section shall prevent a duly authorized representative of any news service, newspaper, or radio or television station or network from entering the area closed pursuant to this section.

Inside the envelope should be a list of previously surveyed evacuation centers, their addresses and capacity. An evacuation center is a location that will provide shelter, toilet facilities, parking space, and property storage. It has been found in most jurisdictions that elementary and junior high schools are excellent evacuation centers. If necessary, evacuation routes may be included from various parts of the community to the designated centers.

The disaster commander must select an evacuation center or centers to be utilized. He must insure that designated persons in charge of these facilities are immediately notified so that they may be opened or otherwise made ready. This notification data is included with the list of evacuation centers. Next, the disaster commander hands the package to the supervisor who will execute the evacuation. The supervisor finds instructions within the package to establish a registry system at the evacuation center. Registration cards may be included in the package but most agencies have found that the regular field interrogation form may be modified for this purpose.

It is essential that all persons evacuated from a disaster area report to the evacuation center and be registered. Registration involves obtaining their name and the address of the residence they abandoned as well as the name, address, telephone number, and other data regarding where they will stay for the duration of the disaster. It may be only through such information that members of families can be reunited, persons may be contacted during the emergency for information regarding their property, and persons may be notified that it is safe to return to the evacuated area. In some cases, the evacuees will remain at the evacuation center. In other cases, they will merely report in, be recorded, and then disperse to other areas. Registration, however, is vitally important, and must be accomplished.

A guideline is also included in the package with respect to using radio and television media for transmission of the evacuation message. Such a guideline must make clear to the supervisor executing the plan the advantages of such notification as well as the peril of panic that it may cause. It should, however, include the media telephone numbers, and a blank model evacuation message form should the supervisor elect to have such a broadcast initiated.

Instructions for putting into operation a survey type evacuation as opposed to a house to house evacuation are included in the package along with the supervisor's responsibility to maintain anti-looting patrols and a complete closure of the evacuated area as well as the department's policy on reentry of a closed area. The system for issuance of re-entry passes and the forms to be used are also included in the package for this supervisor. Many agencies have found that traffic citations may be altered for use as passes in controlling the reentry of persons into a closed area.

Resource Annex

In addition to the previously described systems the disaster commander should have at the tips of his fingers a listing or directory of people and equipment that may be needed during emergencies. Most police departments maintain such a list for their routine operations. With such a list, the disaster commander can quickly obtain the services of a welder, a scuba diver, someone who can communicate with deaf mute children through sign language, a seventy foot aluminum ladder, four flood lights and a gasoline mobile generator, three hundred blankets, etc.

Training for Testing the Plan

Again the true test of the effectiveness of a disaster response plan or its systems is how it functions during a disaster. However, personnel may be trained and tested during simulation, just as with the organization and function plan. Simulation gaming with the disaster response plan, however, must be made far more realistic than is the case with the organization and function plan. This simulation game is played by patrolmen, supervisors, and unit or watch commanders only, as they are the ones most involved in emergency response. Authentic simulations must duplicate the radio communications system, telephone system, and must realistically control time limitations and numbers of personnel participating. (See Appendix G, Chap. 8.)

COMMAND POSTS

The topic of command posts is included under the general subject of planning because much can be done in advance of a disaster to provide an effective command post. In effect, the design, purchase and equipping of a command post or an "emergency operation center" is a part of the planning process just as is determining the duties and responsibilities of the staff that will man it.

Command Post Theory

It has been found through painful experience that disasters, unusual occurrences, riots, and special events require extreme management concentration. In order to establish the level of concentration necessary for successful operations, a divided command must occur in the police agency. One commander must continue to operate the department in all of its normal functions, while the disaster commander must concentrate his efforts, manpower, and equipment solely on the incident.

In the necessary separation of departmental activities that occur, the disaster commander forms a separate organization, his headquarters become a command post, or as it is sometimes called, an "emergency operations center." This theory is also utilized in some of the more routine police operations where it maximizes effectiveness, for example, wilderness searches for missing persons and extensive urban searches for missing children.

Command Post Models

There are three basic types or styles of command posts: a) at the police station—separate from the regular headquarters, b) a mobile unit at the scene, c) a fixed post at the scene. The criteria for establishing a command post at the police headquarters have much to do with the nature of the incident. A disaster which affects the entire community such as an earthquake or general flooding, and where there is no necessity or possibility of establishing a command post at the scene, is probably best commanded from the central police headquarters. Where command posts are established at police headquarters, they are usually separated from regular police operations and housed in separate rooms or basement locations.

Mobile command posts are primarily used for incidents which are isolated within the community such as a fire, an airplane crash or an explosion, and where a command post must be set up quickly and perhaps moved from time to time. A fixed on-scene command post is established where control must be executed at the location of the disaster, but for an extensive length of time, and where large numbers of personnel are involved or weather conditions require more extensive shelter. Fixed command posts are set up in barns, abandoned buildings, and in many cases portions of a business or homes are closed to make room for the command post. Occasionally combinations of mobile and fixed command posts are used at the scene of a disaster where, for example, the mobile unit is parked outside a high school auditorium, the mobile unit is utilized for communication purposes while the auditorium houses the planning and reporting functions, briefing of disaster workers, and equipment storage.

Mobile Command Post Requirements

Mobile command posts are most frequently created by conversion of a commercial bus, truck, or trailer. From agency to agency the requirements may differ depending on the planned use of the mobile command post. Some rural law enforcement agencies combine the supply function within the command post

Police Disaster Planning

and extensive space and compartmentalization for the storage of field type equipment is provided. This equipment includes flashlights, shotguns, batons, helmets, rope, portable barricades, flares, foul weather gear, water, emergency food rations, and other items. The theory is that during an emergency these items of field equipment could not be collected quickly or some might be omitted. By having the items stored in the mobile command post they will be instantly at hand if needed. Because of the rural nature of these agencies, supply centers are usually a considerable distance from the location of emergency incidents, making the transportation of supplies a time consuming process. Thus, they feel well justified in making the mobile command post a limited emergency supply center.

Mobile command posts are usually converted trailers or buses, extensively furnished with communications equipment. (Photo Credit—Florida Highway Patrol)

The primary purpose of a mobile command post, however, is management, not supply. It has been observed that frequently requiring the unit to fulfill both functions limits its effectiveness in each. Agencies which have experienced this problem are beginning to create equipment and supply trailers which are kept fully loaded and which may be towed to the scene of a disaster, thus gaining maximum room within the mobile command post for the management function.

In any event, the minimum requirements for a mobile command post may be grouped under six general areas: utility, electrical, communications, control, management, and staff services. Utility requirements provide for both comfort and security. The unit should be completely air tight and air conditioned. It may have to operate in areas where tear gas has been used during riots or it may suddenly become down-wind of a fire or toxic chemical leak. A public address system as well as an intercom system must be provided so that members of the command post staff may communicate clearly with each other from station to station within the command post and call for various personnel or issue instructions through an outside speaker. The unit should be sound-proofed so that it may be closed up if necessary and communications, planning or briefing may be carried on without disruption. Minimum provisions for coffee, drinking water, and a toilet should be provided within the unit. The unit should be distinctively marked from the top so that it may be identified from the air.

Two electrical systems must be provided in the unit, one which is a power hookup from an established source, and the other is a self-contained generator, powerful enough to operate all communications and lighting equipment within the unit. Whenever possible, the emergency command post will be plugged in to a regular electrical source for power. Under some field conditions, or where a power failure occurs, the mobile command post must be able to generate enough electricity to maintain its own operation. In addition, there should be electrical outlets on the command post so that extension cords and floodlights or other electrical devices may be operated outside the command post.

Another requirement involves communications. This area will contain the radio, radio phone, and telephone equipment deemed necessary for the unit. Generally, the unit should have transmitters and receivers for its regular police frequency, the frequencies of expected mutual aid departments, including sheriffs and state police, and such fire, civil defense or military frequencies as are deemed necessary. Provision for regular telephone hook-up must be built into the unit, as this is frequently necessary where the command post is maintained beyond four to six hours. The communications officer in the command post must be able to communicate by radio with every unit operating in the area of the disaster. As this varies from area to area, it is impossible to provide a complete list of the number and types of transmitters or receivers or monitors required.

Located near the communication center in the command post should be the situation control area. In addition to being adjacent to the communications area, officers manning this post should have an open window or counter to the outside to receive information directly from field personnel. This post maintains the chronological disaster log, maintains and updates situation maps of the disaster, and where desirable, maintains a unit control system which shows the location of all police cars or details in the area. This portion of the command post must provide room for maps, mapboards, chalkboards, and cork boards for messages.

The disaster commander's portion of the command post should be mutually accessible to the communications and situation control areas but should provide him with as much privacy as possible to prevent distraction. It should be designed to provide enough room for small planning conferences and briefing sessions.

The last section of the command post is reserved for staff support functions. Here are provided sufficient desks and tables for use by the press liaison officer, the personnel officer, the intelligence officer, and liaison officers from other jurisdictions or the military. These positions should also have outside windows or counters to facilitate communication with reporting personnel.

The size and design of these areas within the command post is dependent upon the size of the vehicle converted and the nature or scope of operations envisioned. Under ideal circumstances, the disaster commander should be able to oversee all other areas of the command post, be instantly accessible to any area requiring his attention, yet be protected in such a way that he is not distracted by routine operations within the command post. This ideal arrangement is seldom attainable.

Station Command Post Requirements

Most of the requirements for a mobile command post are applicable to the station command post as well as the fixed command post, and here various economies may be effected. If care is used in building the mobile command post, and if its fixtures are made portable, they may be disconnected and moved inside the police station or into a fixed command post at the scene of the disaster. Under this system, an area is designated within the police station which is to be used for emergency command post operations and various tables and other furniture are designated or stored for use. When a disaster occurs, the needed furniture is moved into the command post area and the mobile command post is stripped of its communications equipment, status, and mapboards or other equipment which is moved inside the police station and set up in the designated command post area. The same system can be used when it is determined necessary to establish a fixed command post at the scene of a disaster.

Larger agencies, however, may maintain a complete emergency command center separate from their regular police headquarters which is fully equipped and may become operational immediately. This is, of course, a luxury obtainable only by the very largest police departments in the country. (See Appendix H, Chap. 8.)

SUMMARY

Only through effective advanced planning can a police department prepare to meet its disaster role effectively. Plans must be developed on two levels: a) an overall departmental organization and response plan to be used during the primary and terminal

Typical emergency operations center located at police headquarters, but separated from routine departmental functions. (Photo Credit—Metropolitan Dade County Public Safety Department)

control phases of a disaster, and b) an emergency response plan to be used by on-duty personnel when disaster strikes. Equally as important as the development of these two types of plans is the training of personnel to work with them and the testing of the plans through simulation and command post exercises. Command post design and development is a part of disaster planning.

4
DISASTER MANAGEMENT

The techniques used by a disaster commander may include some or all of those listed in this chapter, depending upon whether or not the incident was a disaster of sudden onset such as an airplane crash, earthquake, explosion, or was a disaster of gradual onset such as rising flood waters or a predictable hurricane. The reader will also notice that much of the material in this chapter is an extension in detail of items mentioned under planning topics.

INITIAL MANAGEMENT

Function of Arriving Officers

The critical duties of the first officers to arrive at a disaster scene cannot be overstated, particularly those nonwarning incidents such as aircraft accidents, earthquakes, explosions, and toxic chemical leaks. Through years of experience the average police officer is conditioned to respond to injured victims, provide first-aid, isolate witnesses, collect evidence, and write reports. It is unfortunate that many cannot free themselves from this conditioning when they are among the first to arrive at a disaster scene. It has been frequently noted that police officers who apply standard police thinking and techniques at disaster scenes often increase the fatality rate, lengthen the treatment time span for victims, and increase the total amount of property damage.

Initial arriving officers must be trained to disregard the injured, ignore the dead, and execute other vital functions before becoming involved in any rescue or first-aid activities. The first officer at the scene must attempt to obtain as complete observation of the disaster as possible. He must not merely view the incident from one position. In some cases, he may have to drive to a number of observation points. Not until the first officer or officers have completely observed the disaster, can they execute the second step which is to estimate the extent, scope, and severity of the disaster and attempt to anticipate additional hazards created by the situation.

The failure to properly and quickly execute these first two functions has complicated disaster response in many nonwarning type incidents. One example occurred in the tornado that struck Michigan in 1955. An early report from a patrol unit advised the Michigan State Police that the center of the tornado impact area was a drive-in theater in the Flint-Beecher area. A responding fire truck was able to proceed past the drive-in theater, and noticed that it had not been badly damaged by the tornado. They did not report this fact, however, and the state police headquarters dispatched many ambulances assuming that there had been heavy casualties at the drive-in theater. Assuming that the direct road was blocked, the ambulances were routed over a number of alternate routes which placed them in a poor response position later when an actual need for them was determined at locations other than the drive-in theater.

After observation and estimation of the extent of the disaster, the third function is prompt and thorough reporting of the incident to headquarters. A police commander of an area involved in a disaster will be waiting to put his emergency response plan into effect. Until he receives a comprehensive and accurate report from the first field units at the scene, he must rely on telephone reports from citizens and others who may not provide accurate and complete information, or under more severe conditions, he may have no other information available due to disruption of the community's telephone service. The reporting officer should not only transmit data regarding severity, scope and extent of the disaster, but should also advise headquarters of other potential hazards created by the disaster and make suggestions regarding road closures, cordoning or evacuation. Finally the officer should stay near the radio following his report so that he will be in a position to answer questions and provide additional information if needed.

Following the execution of these functions, the first officer to arrive at the scene must exercise command over survivors and volunteers to initiate self-help and first aid activities. It must be realized that much of the early effective work in life saving and property protection will be done by volunteers and victims affected by the disaster. For example, in the Beecher tornado over three-quarters of the dead and injured had been removed by civilian volunteers before an emergency command post had been established. Over one thousand civilian volunteers were helping to search and clear the devastated area by the time the disaster commander arrived on the scene. A similar situation was reported in the Worcester tornado.

Volunteer workers are not too effective and may actually be working at cross purposes in some situations, or even worsen a situation by conducting such activities as improper debris removal. In almost every case studied, volunteers and survivors reported themselves to the uniformed officers arriving on the scene, and expected coordination and supervision. The police or fire uniform, coupled with calm demeanor, labels the responding officer as a leader. His proper response is to organize and direct volunteer disaster workers toward productive ends.

The four primary functions of the first officers at the scene of a disaster are observation, estimate of the situation, reporting or communications, and on-scene command. Only if these four functions have been completely and thoroughly executed should arriving officers become involved in actual life saving first-aid or other related activities.

As supervisors or a designated disaster commander arrive on the scene, those officers first to arrive must brief them on changes in the situation and activities that have been initiated. The first supervisor on the scene must verify that the four primary functions have been executed thoroughly, accurately, and verify any changes in the situation. The supervisor should then select one of the first officers to arrive and ask him to chronologically list in his notebook the sequence of events including all steps that have been taken up until this point. The supervisor should then command this officer to accompany him during the initial disaster control operation and keep a running log in his notebook of all occurrences. This activity constitutes the beginning of the disaster log which will be discussed in a following segment.

The supervisor should consult at once with the designated disaster commander regarding the desirability of location of mobile or on-scene fixed command post. The nature of the disaster may require a command post at the location or it may be of such a nature that the disaster commander would elect to conduct management functions from an emergency control center at the police station.

Convergence

The problem of convergence is discussed under initial management techniques because it occurs soon after the occurrence of a disaster and unless steps are immediately taken, it will complicate every following phase of disaster management. In almost all of the disaster cases studied, except those where routes of travel were severed by floors or earthquake damage, the flow of mass numbers of the public toward the disaster scene has constituted an obstacle to control. By such convergence, either on foot or in vehicles the public impedes the flow of fire, police, and rescue vehicles, endangers themselves with respect to disaster related hazards; and create evacuation, crowd control, and looter prevention problems for the police.

It must be understood that the public creates convergence problems from a variety of motives. Some are people who live in the disaster area and are attempting to return to determine damage to their property or family. Others have relatives or personal property in the area and are anxious to survey damage or be reunited. Some are helpers and wish to offer their services if needed. Most are curious and come into the area solely to take pictures and view damage. A few are exploiters who enter the area to become involved in looting or to offer various services for highly inflated prices.

A disaster commander should consider several techniques with respect to disaster convergence. First he should attempt to cordon the disaster at its perimeters, blocking streets and sidewalks, closing freeway or turnpike off-ramps to divert traffic, and insuring that the entrance and exit routes to be used by the fire, police, and rescue personnel are sealed in such a way to speed arrival and departure of disaster related vehicles. Doing this requires personnel and inevitably it cannot be accomplished fully until some time after the impact of the disaster. Yet, an early start at selected locations will usually reduce the total amount of convergence with which he must later cope.

The disaster commander's second consideration is the problem of the "sigalert" or news media notification. In the southern California area, the "sigalert" is a police broadcast to major radio networks. Messages are tape recorded for rebroadcast over these commercial radio stations to notify the public regarding traffic problems, disasters, and other situations which could affect a substantial portion of the population. In addition a part of the disaster response plan for a police department should consist of a notification system which provides for news media notification. The disaster commander should carefully consider this news media notification or "sigalert" with respect to its effect on convergence. There is a possibility that large numbers of persons who would be otherwise unaware of a disaster may learn of it through the news media and become involved in a convergence problem. This hazard must be balanced with the fact that perhaps a substantial number of citizens will avoid the area if they are forewarned of the disaster situation. The disaster commander's knowledge of the past performance of the local population in similar instances should be depended upon, and it is conceivable that he may in some situations wish to delay his news media notification until the cordon of the disaster is more complete.

Additionally the disaster commander should carefully consider open requests for assistance through the news media. During the Flint-Beecher tornado, rescue workers urgently needed flashlights. A radio broadcast for flashlights by a local radio station resulted in approximately five hundred people driving five hundred cars, each carrying no more than one flashlight, into an already congested disaster area. In other disaster cases similar requests for blood donors to respond to hospitals or for doctors to

Disaster Management

respond to train wrecks have resulted in worsening convergence problems and rarely have been effective in accomplishing their objective.

The third technique with respect to convergence is to channel the flow of the public through the area. This channeling process may be undertaken after the disaster is sufficiently under control to prevent further hazard and when sufficient personnel have been assembled to accomplish it. The technique involves establishing a route through the disaster area so that the public may view the damage and then organizing a one-way caravan of the curious through the area. This relieves pressure on the cordon points, satisfies public curiosity, preserves police public relations, but it does utilize precious manpower and is rarely possible to implement during the early stages of a disaster.

Almost every jurisdiction has laws or ordinances to prevent sightseeing, for example under Penal Code section 402, California law states:

> Every person who goes to the scene of a disaster or stops at the scene of a disaster for the purpose of viewing the scene or the activities of policemen, firemen, other emergency personnel, or military personnel coping with the disaster in the course of their duties during the time it is necessary for emergency vehicles or such personnel to be at the scene of the disaster or to be moving to or from the scene of the disaster for the purpose of protecting lives or property, unless it is part of the duties of such person's employment to view such scene or activities, and thereby impedes such policemen, firemen, emergency personnel or military personnel in the performance of their duties in coping with the disaster, is guilty of a misdemeanor.
>
> For the purposes of this section, a disaster includes a fire, explosion, an airplane crash, flooding, windstorm damage, a railroad accident, or a traffic accident.

Experienced disaster commanders soon learn that such laws are virtually unenforceable. During the early stages of disaster control there are not sufficient police to effect arrests or transport prisoners. In addition, evidence that disaster workers' activities were actually impeded must be presented during trials, as well as evidence that the defendant went to the scene of the disaster or stopped there for the "purpose of viewing." This involves the issuance of subpoena as to a multitude of disaster workers with the related time loss and expense. It has further been found that a successful defense on the part of the defendant may be presented if he alleges that he stopped to aid or give assistance. It has thus been found not too effective to arrest or prosecute sightseers at the scene of a disaster.

The Disaster Commander

The officer designated by higher authority, or mandated by department plans or policy, who assumes responsibility and authority for management of the disaster is referred to as the "disaster commander." As he assumes command during the initial management phase, and before involving himself in other control techniques, he should probably seek answers to the following questions.

1. Has *type* of disaster been determined?
2. Has *exact location* been determined?
3. Has *range* been determined?
4. Has medical assistance been initiated?
5. Has command post been established?
6. Has headquarters been kept informed?
7. Have hazards been identified, located, and reported?
8. Have available manpower been assigned?
9. Have equipment requisitions been made?
10. Have personnel needs been reported?
11. Have assignments been recorded?

COMMAND POST MANAGEMENT

After the primary on-scene management functions have been completed by the disaster commander, he must establish a suitable headquarters and develop an organizational staff for the balance of the operation. This headquarters is referred to as a command post, emergency control center, emergency operation center, or field headquarters. However, it is most commonly referred to as a command post. As described under the previous chapter on disaster planning, command posts are generally three types. The first type is a mobile self-equipped command post which may be brought to the scene and may be moved as necessary. The second is a fixed on-scene command post, where a suitable building may be found near the location of the disaster and required equipment installed. The third type of command post is maintained at police headquarters, but is entirely separate from the regular law enforcement operation.

If one of the two types of on-scene command posts is selected by the disaster commander, he should designate its location in line with the following criteria. The command post should be located close enough to the disaster area so that valuable time is not wasted in movement of personnel, messengers, and vehicles between the command post and the disaster scene. By the same token, the command post must not be so close to the scene that the disaster or relief operations create confusion, noise, smoke, or other distractions. The command post should be located on a road net which provides easy access by vehicles, yet this acccess must be controlled to prevent convergence problems from affecting the command post operation. To this end the command post is best secluded from public view, but this concealment must be tempered by the opposing need for disaster workers to be able to locate it quickly and conveniently. In addition, the command post must be located in such a position that there is ample parking for a multitude of vehicles. It should also be located near some existing toilet facilities, and where there is adequate lighting and electrical outlets.

The location selected for the command post probably cannot meet all these criteria. Some must be sacrificed to obtain others, but in many recent instances elementary and junior high school facilities have been found ideal for command post activities, provided school has been dismissed.

Personnel Assignments

After establishment of the command post, the disaster commander will probably begin to delegate some of the management functions, the most important of which will be his selection of a "personnel officer." It is the duty of the personnel officer to immediately begin a manpower control log which he will probably assign to a patrolman to maintain. All personnel responding to the disaster, including those from other agencies, are directed to report to the command post or other location if the personnel officer must move his operation. On reporting, each officer's name, organization or department and disaster assignment is logged as well as the time at which he reported. This information will later permit verification and relief of officers, establishes a planning guide for feeding and other required services, and documents the response or presence of the officer for legal purposes, should he become missing, killed or injured during the disaster operation.

As soon as all the required work assignments at the disaster have been filled, the personnel officer establishes a manpower pool and a waiting area. Responding personnel are assigned to and kept in the waiting area so that when needed they may be rapidly assigned. It is the duty of the personnel officer to supply the disaster commander with sufficient manpower to meet the disaster commander's need during changing phases of the operation.

In the later stages of the disaster, adequate manpower will have been assembled and it is the duty of the personnel officer to select those personnel at the disaster scene who should be relieved from duty. Officers who have been on duty for overly long periods of time, officers from other jurisdictions who have responded under mutual aid agreements, and officers whose primary skills are needed for routine police operations in the community should be considered for relief. Relief personnel are assigned by the personnel officer from his manpower pool.

One additional technique utilized by personnel officers at the scene of some disasters is controversial. It has occurred in the past that there may be an over response by law enforcement personnel. When this occurs, many police officers are actually sightseeing, and not involved in disaster operations. Others respond to the disaster scene and assume a position of responsibility but have never reported to the command post and their presence is unknown. For this reason, personnel officers have occasionally left the command post with a copy of the manpower log and toured the entire disaster scene carrying a supply of distinctive arm bands. Every police officer at the scene of the disaster is identified by the personnel officer, and verified with the manpower log. If he has checked in to the command post and is properly listed and assigned, he is given an arm band and his verification is recorded on the log. If his name cannot be found on the log, one of two things may be done: the personnel officer records his name and agency, and advises the officer that his response is appreciated but that he is no longer needed at the scene and that his agency will be sent a letter of appreciation for his response showing that he was released from duty at a given time. This friendly contact will usually cause the officer to return to his own jurisdiction or organization immediately. The other course of action is followed where the officer in question is executing a required function at the disaster. In this case, the personnel officer enters his name on the manpower log, along with his newly discovered function and the time at which the responding officer claims to have reported to the scene. He is then issued an arm band. After several periodic tours of a disaster scene by the personnel officer he can be fairly certain that he has identified all officers present and he can instantly recognize one who may not have been listed on his log by the absence of an arm band. When this technique is employed, arm bands are issued at the command post to all personnel who are reporting and who are logged in at that location.

The disaster commander should insure that the disaster log is maintained by appointing a command post historian or "log officer." This officer will maintain a chronological listing of significant events that have occurred during the disaster. The importance of such a log will be discussed later in this chapter. The log officer should seek out first officers and supervisors on the scene to attempt to learn from them or from their notes the times and locations that various activities occurred. Note that this log keeping activity should occur beginning with the first officers to arrive at the scene, and certainly with the first supervisor at the scene as previously indicated in this chapter.

As soon as the disaster commander becomes aware that a press notification has been made through the routine notification system of his emergency response plan or upon his sigalert order, he should consider the appointment of a "press liaison officer." Here the disaster commander should attempt to select a supervisor who is congenial, well-spoken, of even temperament, and who has some previous public relations experience. It is the duty of the press liaison officer to immediately tour the disaster scene, develop a realistic assessment of the area, scope and extent of the disaster, the number of fatalities and injuries, the number of responding public safety personnel, the types of equipment used, and time estimates as to containment. In addition, he should attempt to develop some verifiable theories regarding the cause or responsibility for the disaster. While conducting this tour and consulting available records, interviewing the first officers at the scene, or studying the disaster log, he should note those portions of the disaster which are easily and safely accessible, those things at the disaster which have photographic significance, and an area where a press briefing or conference may be held with suitable photographic backgrounds.

Personnel at the disaster scene should be instructed not to give any information to the press. They should be advised to refer all news media representatives to the press liaison officer for briefing. This is vitally important as it has happened frequently that reporters from one media will interview a police officer who describes tremendous damage or vast casualties as he sees it from his side of the disaster, while a reporter from another media will interview a police officer from another side of the disaster who will paint quite a routine picture. Thus in two competing newspapers, or on two competing television stations, entirely different versions of the disaster will be presented to the public. When such embarrassing situations occur, the media tends to blame the police. This can be avoided if all representatives of the news media are required to get their information from one individual specifically equipped for this purpose, the press liaison officer. The information can be more quickly obtained, will be more accurate, and will be more uniform if provided to the press in this manner.

The press liaison officer then responds to the location he has selected for briefing representatives from the news media. As they arrive, he conducts briefing sessions, updated by conferences with the log officer, the situation officer, and other resources. The area selected by the press liaison officer for briefing should be near existing telephone communications if possible, because many radio stations tend to call for a live report from the scene which should also be handled by the press liaison officer.

Periodically the press liaison officer will take those members of the news media who desire it, on a tour of the disaster area. He will conduct them over pre-planned routes which enable them to obtain the best view and photographs of the scene, but which keep them from interfering with the disaster operations. He calls attention to certain significant or highly photographic features and his continual presence acts as a buffer to prevent altercations between eager reporters and exhausted disaster workers.

The disaster commander will probably appoint an "intelligence officer" or a situation officer as he is sometimes called. It is the responsibility of this officer to continually follow the status or progress of operations ordered by the disaster commander, to attempt to predict future occurrences, manpower requirements or supply needs, and to maintain a constant evaluation of available resources. The disaster commander cannot keep track of these details as he is involved in the making of continual operational decisions. The quality of these decisions is greatly enhanced if he can turn to his intelligence officer at any time and get an immediate briefing on the elements of the problem involved. It is further the duty of the intelligence officer to advise the disaster commander periodically of the necessity for making certain decisions which range from the routine, such as organizing the relief system so that on-duty officers may be fed or attempting to predict how many officers will be needed during the next twenty-four to thirty-six hours, to such critical decisions such as preventing the disaster commander from committing manpower to a convergence problem when it is evident that the same manpower will be needed in thirty to forty-five minutes to conduct an evacuation from a threatened area.

These staff positions (personnel, log, press, and intelligence) are usually the minimum with which a disaster commander can function. He may appoint a number of other staff officers and delegate special functions to them, depending on the size of the operation and its duration. These additional positions will be discussed later under their functional headings, for example, evacuation control officer, ambulance dispatch officer, and property control officer.

Chronological Log

The maintenance of a disaster log is vital to the success of the operation. This log is used continually by the disaster commander and the intelligence officer in their activities, and becomes particularly important to insure follow-up on action that has been instituted. Depending upon the extent or duration of the disaster, the amount of delegation authorized by the disaster commander, and the number of self-executing systems incorporated into the disaster response plan, the log may be more or less detailed. For example, a detailed log might include a chronological listing of all activities from the initial notification of the disaster including inquiries from every source, the dispatching of personnel, the transmitting and receiving of radio messages, the arrival of equipment or various staff officers, mutual aid personnel, orders given by the disaster commander, the content of any sig-alerts or proclamations issued, and the time and location of every incident during the disaster including the location of and identity of any bodies found, time of closure of certain areas, and time of completion of evacuations.

Usually, however, the disaster log concerns only the activities occurring within the disaster, and other systems or logs are utilized for the documenting of specialized information. The notification system will document those persons notified, the time, and the message given them. The personnel officer's manpower log will document the arrival of personnel on the scene and their assignment. A time indexed recording tape connected to the communication section of the command post will document radio messages, their content, and time. With this auxiliary system of logs, the main disaster log may be reserved solely for those incidents concerning the disaster.

The disaster log assumes even greater importance after the entire operation is completed. It becomes a primary information source for insurance companies in the settling of claims on both public and private property which has been damaged or destroyed, may be subpoenaed in law suits to determine liability for damages during the disaster, and it may be used by public safety personnel to defend their actions and document their response and attempts at life saving or disaster control. It becomes important in post-operational critiques and in the development of new or altering of present disaster response plans. (See Appendix I, Chap. 8.)

Control Problems

One of the most vexing problems in command post management is keeping track of who has been assigned to do what, who is available for assignment, what is the status of an on-going assignment, how many men are assigned to which assignment, or being supervised by whom. It is impossible for the intelligence officer, much less the disaster commander, to keep these facts in mind, and it is cumbersome to attempt to get this information from the disaster log each time it is needed to make an operational decision.

The problem of control is greatly simplified by the use of one or more "status" boards. These are usually best made of magnetized metal, finished as chalkboards. Metal backed placards made of chalkboard material and large enough for the listing of names or equipment items, perhaps furnished in a variety of colors, are used in connection with the board.

An example of its use would be as follows: the disaster commander orders the evacuation of twenty-five homes threatened by a brush fire, the intelligence officer lists the evacuation order and location on one line of the chalkboard. He then obtains a supervisor and a number of officers from the manpower pool at

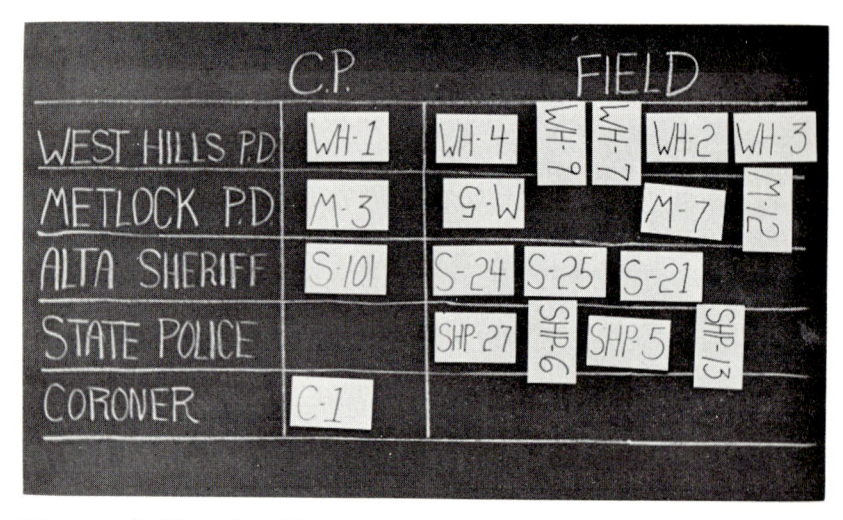

Magnetic chalkboard enables command-post personnel to determine status of units participating in disaster control. Magnetic placards are rotated to indicate availability or assignment. (Photo credit—R. L. Throne.)

the discretion of the personnel officer. The names of the supervisor and the patrolmen are written on a red placard. The red placard is placed next to the assignment on the magnetized chalkboard in an upside down position to show that they have been dispatched. Its color indicates that the agency's own personnel are handling the evacuation, and that they may be reached on the agency's radio frequency. When the evacuation team arrives in the area and begins the evacuation, the placard is rotated showing that they are in the process of completing the assignment. The moment the evacuation team confirms that the operation is completed, the placard is rotated again signifying the team is enroute to the command post or to another assignment. When the team reports back to the personnel officer and are reassigned to the manpower pool, the placard is removed and the assignment is marked as completed. It may then be erased from the magnetic chalkboard as soon as it is verified that the log officer has logged the operation and has recorded the various times involved.

Other colored placards might be used for state police or county sheriff's units if it is necessary for communications purposes or

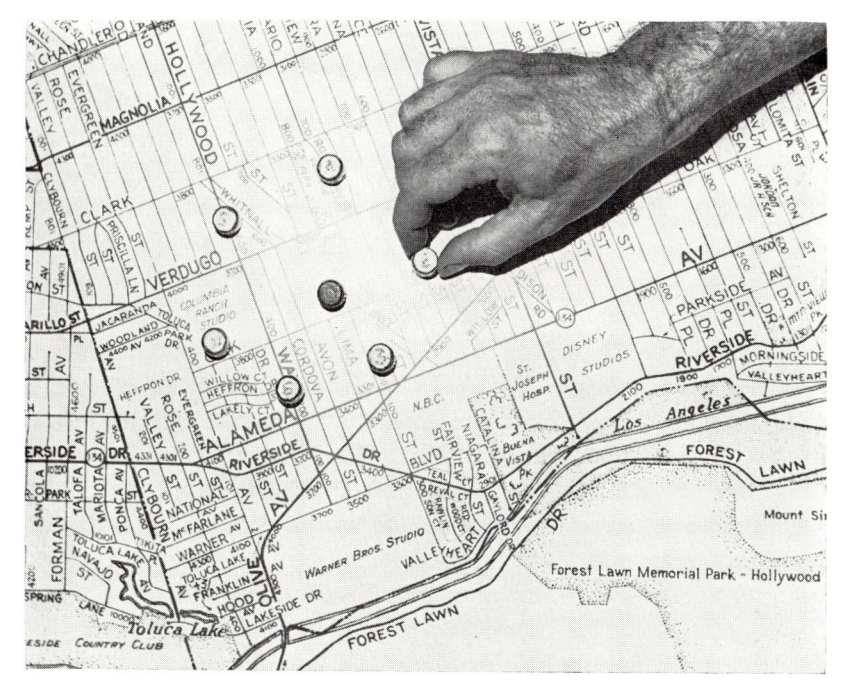

Magnetic map board permits command-post personnel to keep track of exact geographical location of units during disaster. (Photo credit—R. L. Throne.)

desirable from the standpoint of other control problems to differentiate these units from the department's own personnel. In small situations, status boards may be used to control patrol cars within a disaster area. In a large disaster operation the status board should be maintained by one officer assigned solely to this task. These boards must be located near the communications center in the command post, and easily accessible to the log officer.

If color coding abbreviations or letter coding are used, not only must all personnel be familiar with the coding, but a statement of the coding must be posted over each board. Another variation of the status board system is the development of magnetized maps. This permits the actual location of assignments or operations to be shown as well as information on the men or equipment accomplishing a given task.

SPECIAL TECHNIQUES

Some problems are common to many disasters, such as evacuation, casualty sorting, body recovery, and recovered property control. From the experiences of a number of agencies, through a wide variety of disasters, certain special techniques have been found successful in meeting these problems. They are presented here in a general fashion to permit innovation and easy adaptation to given situations.

Closure and Evacuation

The legal authority to close an area or evacuate the residents from a neighborhood varies from state to state. California's Penal Code section 409.5 is cited in the chapter on planning. Under this law, the disaster commander, declaring a given area to be a "disaster area," may order that it be cordoned off and that no persons except the press may enter without police permission. He may also order all persons within the area to leave. Their failure to do so constitutes an offense, and they may be arrested and transported from the area if necessary.

Evacuations are generally of two types: emergency and urgent. In an emergency evacuation, no time exists to close and cordon the area, to establish evacuation routes, locate and plan for the removal of pets and livestock, or verify the locking and security of business and residences. In an emergency evacuation, there exists only time enough for officers to saturate the area with public address systems, advising the residents that they must leave the area at once. How this warning should be given depends very much on the nature of the disaster. If the danger is approaching from a particular direction, it would be most important to notify those persons first who are in the most hazardous position. If at all possible during an emergency evacuation officers should advise residents of the designated evacuation center and order them to report there at once after leaving the closed area.

Urgent evacuations can be carried out in a much more thorough and effective manner, because extreme haste is not necessary. The disaster commander, after ordering the evacuation, then determines or instructs the supervisor charged with the operation to determine the limits of the evacuation, and the evacuation center to which the residents must report. An evacuation officer is assigned to that center to verify that it is in readiness and to log in evacuees as they arrive. The area to be evacuated is first cordoned to prevent reentry. Evacuation routes from the area are selected, designated, and cordoned. An evacuation message is drafted and is broadcast to residents by public address system, and over all pertinent radio and television stations. This message should designate the area concerned in the evacuation. It should advise the residents of the reason for the evacuation, it should advise them if they are to walk or drive their own car out, how much personal property they may take with them, what items it would be desirable for them to bring such as blankets, portable radios, and precious small possessions. The message should also identify the evacuation center, stress the importance of their reporting in, and perhaps the route that they should follow to that center. Other instructions such as reporting the location and type of pets abandoned, locking their homes and turning off utilities should also be included.

Officers saturate the area with this message for a reasonable period of time, alternately using their sirens or other attention getting devices. After a period of time commensurate with the size of the area and number of evacuees involved, a team of inspection officers begin in one sector or corner of the area to be evacuated. They search each street, knock on doors, verify that businesses are secure, and that all residents have left the area. This inspection sweep must be done sector by sector, and each sector that has been verified must be blocked off to prevent evacuees from reentering. Persons who resist evacuation should be arrested and transported if law permits.

Finally, the inspection teams will have cleared the entire evacuation area up to the original cordon. It now becomes the responsibility of the evacuation officer to maintain security patrols within the area to the extent that it is safe for police officers to function there. These security officers are watchful for hazards to property, such as fire and looting. Only the evacuation officer should determine which persons may reenter the area. Usually authorized press representatives are permitted to enter the area but are usually given a police escort. If it becomes necessary for evacuees to reenter the area for a period of time, they should be given an easily recognizable pass which should designate the exact location to which they should be admitted and the amount of time that they may stay.

All evacuees should report to the evacuation center. Where evacuees have not been permitted to drive their cars out of the area and have been mass transported by bus, this is quite simple to control. The more independent method used for evacuation, the less success is obtained in having all evacuees register at the center. The evacuation center control officer must log all evacuees. Under some circumstances, evacuees will stay at the center. Under most circumstances, however, they will merely report in and then will leave to live with relatives, acquire quarters in a motel or hotel, or various other arrangements.

In registering, they must list each person that has been evacuated from the area, that is, each member of a family or household, and must designate where they can be reached or will be staying. This is important for a number of reasons. It has frequently occurred that where an area has been evacuated for any period of time it becomes necessary for fire, utility, police, or other emergency services to contact the owner of a residence or business regarding some hazard or problem. Unless it is known where they are staying during the evacuation, this is impossible and it may complicate disaster relief work.

Registration becomes essential in the reuniting of families, particularly where children are concerned, and a great load can be removed from the juvenile detail of the police department or the school district if the parents of children can be readily located. In a recent major fire, for example, the police were required to evacuate some six hundred residents from a raging brush fire at 1:00 in the afternoon. The children of these residents attended elementary and junior high schools some distance away in an area unaffected by the fire. The endangered area was promptly and thoroughly evacuated, and no sooner had this been accomplished than school buses began to arrive at the road blocks cordoning the evacuated area. Agitated school bus drivers demanded to know what they should do with the children. The school buses were dispatched to the evacuation center and parents were contacted to pick up their children.

When an area previously evacuated is to be reopened, the evacuation officer should attempt to organize the return by segments or sectors. Otherwise, a situation much resembling the "Oklahoma land rush" will occur and traffic congestion, coupled with the fatigue and discomfort of the evacuees, may create altercations and disturbances requiring more police action.

Rescue from Debris

This type problem occurs where buildings or other structures have collapsed due to explosions, earthquakes, construction faults, or tornados, and it is feared that a number of victims are trapped in the rubble and debris. While their removal is essentially a rescue operation executed by the fire department and other emergency services, the police are often involved in the first few stages of this operation.

During World War II, the British civil defense services developed some highly successful techniques for the rescue of victims from debris, and the disaster commander will find that if he begins using these techniques the fire and other rescue services may easily take over the operation when appropriate. It is found that rescue operations where victims are trapped in rubble and debris are most effective when carried out in four stages. The first stage involves an immediate survey of the surface and surrounding areas of the disaster. Victims who are clearly visible are removed and transported or directed to the ambulance dispatch post or other medical services facility. Before they are permitted to be removed, however, rescue intelligence is conducted. If the victim is conscious, he is asked who else was with him at the time of the incident, how many others were in the building at the time of the incident, and interrogated regarding the whereabouts of persons in nearby buildings. By collecting rescue intelligence at this point, the first officers on the scene may learn where a concentrated search should be conducted and verify collapsed buildings that need not be searched immediately.

The second stage involves disaster workers entering the collapsed structures and attempting to locate those survivors who are not visible from the street, but may be reached without entensive debris removal—in basements, under stair wells, or in voids created by collapsing roofs. Again, before these victims are released or transported for medical treatment, rescue intelligence must be conducted and they are asked questions similar to those in stage one. The police may well be expected to be involved in stage one and stage two. By the time stage three must be started there are usually sufficient fire, utility, engineer, and rescue personnel available to release the police from this task.

The third stage of rescue consists of the removal of selected debris in areas where it is reasonably assumed that survivors may exist. The locations where this is conducted are often dependent upon the rescue intelligence gathered during stage one and stage two. The final stage consists of complete rubble clearance, systematically sifting through the collapsed area from one edge to the other. This is done when there are victims still unaccounted for during the first three stages of rescue or where there is any possibility of survivors being trapped.

The police are occasionally involved in the fourth stage when bodies are discovered and when they are charged with the task of body removal or identification. Police are additionally involved where rescue workers recover valuable property and there is no owner immediately available to claim it. In these cases it is the responsibility of the police to recover, record, and store a variety of types of property.

Casualty Sorting

The casualty rate in a disaster has often been increased by improper transportation of victims or failure to institute any system of priority for medical treatment. An illustration of this problem occurred when a light plane crashed into a grandstand during an air show. Eleven persons were killed and forty others received serious injuries. Fire and police rescue workers were able to remove the injured safely and conveniently to the north side of the endangered grandstand, but ambulances could respond only to the south side. Stretcher bearers were required to spend at least twenty minutes per victim carrying the injured around the grandstand. Once loaded, each ambulance driver proceeded to the nearest emergency hospital. The nearest hospital, not having been notified of the disaster, accepted the first few ambulance loads of victims. When the third ambulance arrived, it was determined by the admitting nurse that the victims could not receive immediate treatment; and after a loss of approximately ten minutes, the ambulance transported its load to the next nearest hospital. Ambulance drivers were not notified over their radios that the first hospital was totally committed. Thus, most of the ambulances leaving the grandstand proceeded to this hospital and had to be re-directed to the next nearest hospital. This fiasco was repeated several times and those victims who were last placed in ambulances spent hours before finally arriving at a major emergency hospital in the nearest metropolitan area. Many of the victims of this incident died of shock and loss of blood, where they might have recovered if given prompt medical attention.

A number of techniques have been developed to expedite treatment of the injured. The first technique is the creation of an emergency hospital radio frequency. Under this system, all ambulances are on the same radio frequency as the major hospitals. Just as soon as one emergency hospital is notified of a disaster, (hopefully by the notification system of the police emergency response plan) that hospital broadcasts an alert to all other hospitals. The admitting authorities of each hospital immediately verify their emergency treatment capacity and this information is relayed to ambulance drivers while they are still en route to the disaster. Thus, each ambulance driver can be directed to a hospital which can accommodate victims on arrival. Further, all ambulances are advised to respond to a designated ambulance dispatch post which is designated by the disaster commander.

An ambulance dispatch post (and there may be several depending on the scope of the disaster) is a location at which victims may be collected and which is easily accessible by ambulance.

It serves as a staging area where ambulances may pick up victims. Where hospitals and ambulances cannot be coordinated in advance, in the manner just described, it becomes necessary for the disaster commander to designate an ambulance dispatch officer at the ambulance dispatch post. All ambulances are instructed to report to the ambulance dispatch post and to pick up victims from no other location. The ambulance dispatch officers then communicate through headquarters, or directly by telephone if possible, with each emergency hospital to verify their admitting room capacity. This data is noted in his notebook. As ambulances arrive and are loaded, he directs the ambulance driver to the hospital which can accommodate them. That hospital's capacity is then readjusted in the officer's notebook, and in this way an attempt is made to insure rapid transportation of victims to hospitals which can provide them with prompt medical treatment.

The creation of a police ambulance dispatch post officer implies that in some disasters "casualty sorting" may be necessary. Casualty sorting is best done by medical personnel. Unfortunately they are rarely at the scene of a disaster during the initial phase when this operation is most important. Therefore, the police officer assigned to the ambulance dispatch post must at least have a general idea of the techniques involved in casualty sorting. The justification for casualty sorting is that when there are a large number of injured persons, the delays caused by ambulance transportation and overcrowded hospital facilities require some victims to be awarded priority for transportation.

It is usually most convenient to sort victims into three classifications. The first consists of those who have minor injuries and who, while they require medical treatment, are in no great danger of death, nor will their condition be greatly worsened by a delay in treatment. This classification receives a secondary priority for transportation. The second classification are those victims whose injuries appear to be terminal or where their injuries are so extensive that they probably would not survive even if they receive medical treatment. This classification is also given a secondary priority for transportation. The third classification, which is given primary priority for transportation, are those persons who appear to have a chance of eventual recovery if they are given prompt medical attention, but whose injuries are severe or extensive.

It is usually found that hospitals which are designated for emergency or disaster utilization have their own system of call-up of medical personnel which they put in operation immediately upon notification. It behooves a watch commander to request designated medical personnel to respond to the ambulance dispatch post as early in the disaster as possible. Here they may conduct casualty sorting far more professionally than can a policeman, and in addition, they may provide emergency first aid prior to ambulance transportation.

It is usually found during a disaster that a hospital survey physician will examine all incoming patients and resort casualties.

Recovery of the Dead

The recovery and identification of the dead is necessary for a number of reasons. While this function is normally carried out by the coroner or medical officer of a county or state, studies of most disasters indicate that the police are closely involved in this function, providing manpower and equipment. In areas where the coroner or medical examiner are "nonprofessional," the police may have to provide the entire system. In some disasters such as earthquakes, tornadoes, and hurricanes, recovery and identification of the dead is simple. The bodies have not been overly mutilated, burned, blown apart, submersed in water for long periods of time, or otherwise disintegrated. However, in airplane crashes, explosions and fires, recovery becomes a matter of piece by piece retrieval and identification is difficult or impossible.

While the dead must be recovered for the usual religious, cultural, and sanitation reasons, there are other aspects that make this function highly necessary. Extreme psychological trauma is experienced by individuals and families who do not know if a loved one is dead or alive. The tragedy of the loss of a loved one is often less traumatic than a long period of uncertainty. Estates must be submitted to probate. Actual proof of death is many times necessary for a widow to claim inheritance or for an insurance company to settle a policy claim. Eventual remarriage of survivors may be complicated. The conducting of business by partnerships and corporations may be complicated. Insurance fraud, civil claims, and information on the actual cause of the disaster may all rely on efficient recovery and identification of the dead.

The recovery of the dead presents some significant problems, and the disaster commander should appoint a "morgue officer." This officer serves to provide liaison between the police service and the coroner or medical examiner. Where body recovery becomes entirely a police function he establishes a system and manages the total recovery operation. His first step is to designate and establish a temporary mortuary or confer with the coroner to select a suitable location. In most disasters, the regular county morgue can be available but is too small. Private mortuaries are usually insufficient to accommodate the number of bodies, and where identification of the dead constitutes a problem, it is almost mandatory that all recovered bodies be kept at the same location.

The location selected for a temporary morgue must be readily accessible to the disaster site, must provide sufficient protected and secluded area for the layout of the bodies, and must provide adequate parking and private conference rooms to accommodate survivors and others visiting the location to make visual identification. In addition, some sort of comfortable seating facility, adequate toilets, and perhaps coffee or other stimulants should be provided as the temporary morgue frequently becomes a gathering place for survivors who are waiting for identification of the dead. In some cases, hundreds of persons will be waiting for up to twenty-four hours under extremely negative psychological conditions.

Police investigative and identification officers should be assigned to work with the coroner or medical examiner in identification of the bodies. Where visual identification cannot be made, or where the body lacks some method of property identification such as wristwatch, billfold or wallet, bracelet, or tattoo, the identification must be made by attempts at fingerprinting, dental charting, and x-ray comparison with prior medical records. The type of identification is time consuming and may take as long as two weeks. In addition, while the FBI disaster squad and local law enforcement identification officers have an outstanding record in the identification of disaster victims, it must be understood that a number of individuals cannot be identified even though finger prints are developed, a dental chart is plotted, and other techniques are utilized. There are many persons in the United States today upon whom there are no fingerprint records, who never visited a dentist, or whose dentist cannot be traced. For these reasons the identification of young children is particularly complicated.

In cases of severe mutilation or extreme burning where fingerprint or medical identification is ineffective, identification of the dead depends to a great extent upon the techniques used in body recovery at the scene which can tie the location of the body to various tools, equipment, other property items, or location. Efficient field recovery techniques are based on a number of established principles. First of all, only a few selected personnel should be involved in field body recovery. These individuals should be carefully briefed on the system to be used, the area should be completely cordoned off, and only the selected authorized recovery workers should be permitted to function in the area.

The area in which the bodies are to be recovered must be geographically segmented into recognizable locations, or grids. For example, in the area of an airplane crash, the entire perimeter wherein bodies may be found is roped off, and then lateral and longitudinal grids are established. Usually kite string or cord is used, although in some instances line marking dust has been borrowed from a local football field. These grids are numbered along one base, the opposite base is labeled by letters. Where an explosion has occurred there is a force direction of the blast and most of the bodies and other property will be found along the force lines, unless the force went in a 360 degree pattern. Where there are definite force lines, a cone shaped grid may be laid out with its apex at the point of explosion. The radial search areas running outward from the apex are numbered and recovery workers establish lettered cross-grids at reasonable distances along the radial lines. In either of these two systems, distinctly identifiable areas are created, for example: 3b, or 5c.

Where the grid system is not practical, a point of reference system is used. In an extremely congested urban center, or in mountainous areas, such things as telephone poles, fire hydrants, light standards, pine trees, boulders, and other permanent objects may be marked with a locator number. Under this system, the body or property would bear a tag with a number of the permanent locator nearest it. It has occasionally been practical to drive numbered stakes where each body is found, particularly in airplane crashes where the location of the body may be of additional investigative assistance to the Federal Aviation Agency.

It is desirable for the recovery workers to photograph in place each body part recovered. Prior to photography, the identification tags should be attached to the body or body part; and since it may not show up on the photograph, a portable chalkboard should be placed beside or behind the body part with the identification number plainly visible. This chalkboard should not be so large, however, that it obscures the terrain near the body.

Where items are found near a body or body part that are obviously related to that body part, they are tagged with the same body recovery number as given to the body. The property which is found in the grid area which is not obviously related to the body is merely tagged with the grid number or locator number. Recovery workers then are concerned with two types of identification: a body number where a body or body part is found and a grid number which is awarded to all bodies, body parts, and all property recovered in the search. Thus, a given body might bear body number 21 and might also bear grid number 5c designating where it was found. Items obviously related to the body are placed in the same body recovery bag with the body, although they are tagged separately. Property items not obviously related to the body are bagged separately and tagged with the grid number. Body recovery bags are usually rubberized canvas, although blankets, mattress covers and a variety of other such devices may be substituted.

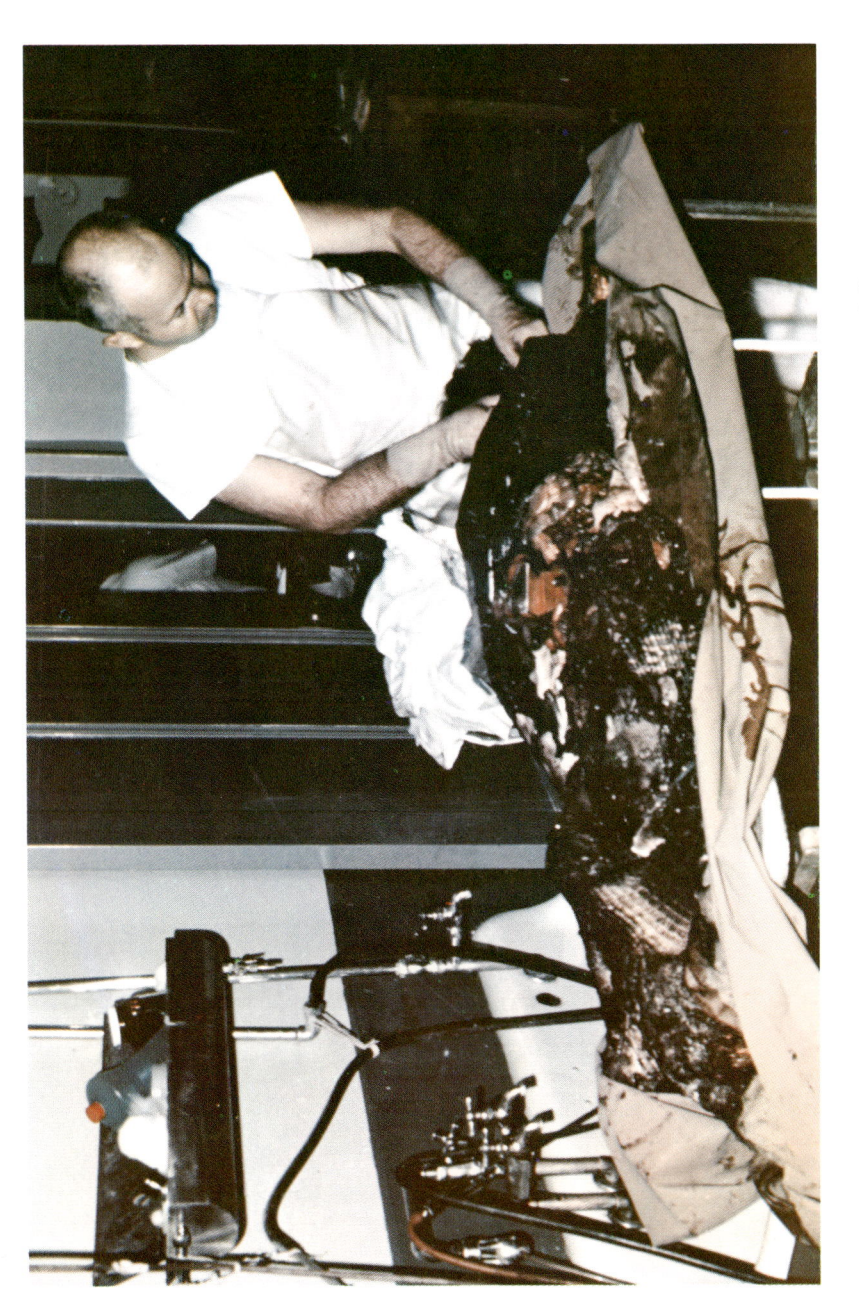

Detailed search of bodies is best left for identification or coroner specialists who may carry out this function in a proper facility.

All bodies, body parts, and significant property are transported to the temporary morgue. At this location sufficient space is available to lay out and record the materials which have been found. A map or chart is made of the disaster area, and the grid system or locator system is entered on the chart. The location of important items is recorded on the chart. In this way, those bodies and body parts not identified at the temporary morgue may be transported later for refrigeration and investigators may still reconstruct the area of recovery.

Handling survivors and relatives at the temporary morgue may present a police public relations problem. Where bodies are not horribly mutilated or burned, visual identification of the dead is possible. This is not suggested, however, where bodies are badly decomposed, burned or mutilated. In these cases, it is suggested that survivors identify property, clothing, or other items recovered with the deceased, and not actually view the body. It is further suggested that survivors not be permitted to remove bodies to private mortuaries until the coroner, medical examiner, or police identification officer in charge of the temporary morgue is satisfied that the particular body in question will not be needed to verify or eliminate the identification of another body. Usually a rule is established that no bodies will be released until a given time. This places the police in a position of releasing no bodies, and no favoritism may be alleged by emotional families.

Mutual Aid Problems

Requesting and assigning mutual aid assistance is a vital disaster control technique in most small and medium-sized police departments. Unless managed properly, it is fraught with hazards. One of the advantages of mutual aid is that in most situations it is the most rapid method of mobilizing manpower. Officers from surrounding jurisdictions can usually be on duty in the disaster area, within a few minutes of the request. Experiments with manpower recall systems show that off-duty and reserve officers take much longer to respond in comparable numbers. One community was, in a recent test, able to recall only fifty per cent of its off-duty and reserve officers within a three-hour period. Thus it becomes obvious that mutual aid officers constitute an important segment of the total manpower available for initial disaster control.

When utilizing mutual aid forces every attempt must be made to relieve them as soon as possible for return to their own jurisdictions. In as much as they responded to the disaster from an on-duty status in their own jurisdiction, it follows that their community is left with limited law enforcement protection as long as they are on disaster duty. A further complication is that should they remain on duty past their normal tour of assignment in their own jurisdiction, that community is responsible for overtime salary. The failure to promptly relieve mutual aid forces for return to their own jurisdiction has created complicated financial claims and an atmosphere which endangers future mutual aid responses.

To prevent these problems from occurring, the disaster commander should assure that mutual aid forces are assigned to perimeter duties so that they can be easily relieved by men from his own department as they become available. In addition, he should insure that mutual aid forces are not assigned to tasks which could cause them injury, property damage, or result in later court subpoenas. In many communities, provision is made for mutual aid forces to respond to the police station and take over many of the internal functions as well as general policing of the uninvolved disaster perimeter.

Another problem with requesting mutual aid assistance occurs where the disaster commander does not specifically include in his request the location to which such forces should respond. Requests for mutual aid should usually omit the location of the disaster, providing instead the location of the command post, the assembly point, or the police station to which these forces should respond. All too frequently, blanket requests for mutual aid have been made during a disaster and neighboring jurisdictions have dispatched numerous police units which have arrived all around the perimeter of the incident and have become involved in disaster relief work which was not coordinated and which was therefore relatively ineffective.

It has been found that police officers from one jurisdiction occasionally are not responsive to orders and directions of supervisors from another jurisdiction during mutual aid operations. For this reason, it is advantageous to request supervisors with mutual aid assistance. On arrival, the mutual aid forces should be assigned to operations where they can work as a unit. Orders should be given to supervisors from the responding agency and these supervisors should be permitted to direct and control the activities of their own officers.

Command Problems

Command problems include those created by internal competition within the police organization for status and authority, as well as the competition between organizations such as fire and police or police and sheriffs, or city police and state police. This competition creates inefficiency during the disaster and almost always results in jealousy, quibbling, recrimination, charges and counter charges, following a disaster.

At one disaster the operation was being commanded by a police lieutenant. A captain arrived on the scene, and advised the lieutenant that he was taking charge. The lieutenant thereupon briefed the captain and he assumed the role of disaster commander. The Assistant Chief for the police department arrived on the scene, and declined to take command, advising the captain that he was merely there as an observer. The County Sheriff arrived on the scene, found it was being commanded by a police captain and advised the captain that since the operation involved both sheriffs and city police personnel, he was assuming the role of disaster commander and relieved the city police captain. The Assistant Chief of police declined to become involved at this point. Later the Chief of police arrived and charged the Sheriff with interference. A confrontation occurred in the presence of numerous public safety personnel which was embarrassing for all concerned.

It is of interest to note that while all this was occurring, the policemen and sheriff's deputies at the scene continued to get most of their directions from the police lieutenant who had first assumed the role as disaster commander. A lawsuit later developed due to the injury of a deputy sheriff who claimed incompetence on the part of the lieutenant and cited his being relieved as disaster commander by the captain and later the sheriff as evidence. In addition, the city declined to pay city policemen overtime for working the disaster, charging that since the sheriff had assumed command of the disaster the policemen had automatically become deputized sheriff's personnel, hence the charge should be upon the county not the city.

Ridiculous situations such as this can have long-lasting negative effects in the day-to-day working relationships of law enforcement and other public safety organizations. They can only be avoided by disaster plans which clearly indicate channels of authority, responsibility, and designation of leadership. Organizational competition following a disaster is generally related to publicity and financing. One method of avoiding post-disaster competition between organizations is to insure that news releases, television specials, radio interviews, and all other methods possible are used to publicize the good work done by all organizations involved in the disaster operation. When credit is liberally and publicly awarded to agencies, it tends to blunt their competitive nature.

Since the mainspring of community government seems to be their financial structure, little can probably be done to prevent post-disaster quibbling over finances. Following the February, 1971 earthquake in San Fernando, the Los Angeles City fire department's union "Fire Fighters Local 112" filed a protest before a sub-committee of the city council charging that the police department was paid 113,000 dollars in overtime, while the fire department only received 9,700 dollars. They charged that they did not receive sufficient overtime, and were forced to eat and sleep under unfavorable conditions. They charged that county firemen were provided with sleeping trailers, but city firemen were required to sleep wherever they could find shelter. It was pointed out during the hearing that the police department faced problems which involved extensive manpower employment for many days during the aftermath of the earthquake, while the fire department operation was over by the evening of the first day.

Perhaps such quibbling could be reduced or prevented by giving adequate "social credit" to public safety agencies involved in disaster response. However, it would seem that such petty animosities and quibbling can only be eliminated from post-disaster operations when the agencies involved in disaster response achieve a true professionalism.

Recovered Property

Some disasters produce a large amount of abandoned or endangered property. Personal effects, luggage, and valuables scattered at the scene of a train wreck, or airplane crash; items of furniture and wearing apparel, abandoned or lost during evacuation; property which has been scattered by hurricane, tornado, and flood; and items which have been removed by looters and abandoned, or recovered during an arrest operation, all constitute the types of recovered property for which the police must become responsible.

Although not a part of initial disaster management, the disaster commander will find that he must eventually create some type of property control system along with other command post operations. This is generally done by appointing a property control officer who places in operation a property storage identification and claim system. While the property storage facilities of the police station may be used for this purpose, they are generally found to be inadequate in size. In addition, the large number of persons who will be attempting to claim property may cause congestion at the police station.

The property control officer usually selects a location separate from the police station and command post, but within the general area of the disaster to establish his property control center. Schools, vacant business buildings, VFW halls, churches, and public utilities storage yards all have been used for this purpose in the past. A system is established whereby each item of recovered property is recorded on a file card by description and serial number, if available. A central claim desk is established where disaster victims may describe their missing property and the claim desk officer attempts to advise the citizen if it has been recovered. The officer then steps into the storage area, examines the property, returns, and asks the citizen for a more complete description.

If the officer is satisfied that the property probably belongs to the citizen, it is released to him. The citizen must provide complete identification and this is entered on the control card for the item. Some departments take a polaroid photograph of the victim with his property to prove return or to identify the citizen should some later ownership dispute occur. The photograph is attached to the control card. All recovered property tagged with the location where it was found, time, date, and other information. This data is occasionally helpful in assisting a disaster victim to claim his property.

During the planning phase the police department will do well to obtain a legal opinion on disaster property control techniques, as they may incur some civil liability during this function. On occasion, insurance adjusters have asked to tour the property storage area. This has created some problems and a suggested technique is to require an insurance claims adjuster to follow the same procedure as individual disaster victims, and in addition to show the claim form submitted by the insured. Whether to release property to an insurance adjuster depends on legal opinions in individual jurisdictions.

POST-OPERATIONAL CRITIQUE

Any law enforcement agency which has just gone through a disaster operation has acquired extensive experience and individual members will doubtless have many ideas on how to improve performance in the future, changes required in disaster plans, and modifications of equipment or techniques. Unfortunately this data is usually lost following a disaster. A post-operational critique attempts to capture this valuable information so that it may be utilized in the future. Such critiques are best conducted immediately after the event, when personnel are a little tired and perhaps angry. In this mood they tend to more freely express their satisfaction or dissatisfaction with procedures, equipment, and techniques.

The long-term nature of police disaster operations usually mandates that some type of continual post-operational critique be conducted as officers will be going on and off duty continually. Therefore it behooves the disaster commander to create the staff position of operational critique officer. This officer contacts the personnel officer, arranges for all personnel being placed off duty to be mustered at some central location, and conducts critiques every few hours. This continual critique system tends to best capture the true feelings of the officers who have been involved in the disaster response. At the conclusion of the disaster operation the critique must be written in journal form so that it may be compared with existing disaster plans and be evaluated with respect to changes in equipment and techniques.

SUMMARY

Disaster management is essentially a matter of determining priorities, recognition of future problems whose solutions must be implemented well in advance, and delegation of routine support duties so that the focus of attention can constantly be upon a situation as it changes. Disaster management is implementation of a disaster plan with innovations to meet changing needs, and applying proven techniques to meet specific problems such as evacuation, casualty sorting, custody of recovered property, and body recovery.

5
DISASTER PSYCHOLOGY

It is of value to the disaster commander to understand some of the psychological reactions of people who have been subjected to the stress of catastrophe. Changes occur under extreme stress situations in both the physical and mental condition of victims as well as disaster workers.

PSYCHOLOGY OF THE VICTIM

At the Time of Warning

In disasters such as flood, hurricanes, forest and brush fires, there is usually an opportunity to give the public some advance warning. The psychological attitudes of those under threat varies considerably. Those persons who are resourceful and are given a plan to follow by public authorities, as well as those persons who have been through a similar disaster under the direction of governmental agencies wherein their property and lives were properly protected, will function reliably. They will show few signs of stress and usually will be able to accomplish the tasks at hand such as preparing for evacuation, hosing down a shingle roof, releasing livestock, or filling containers with water.

The psychological reaction of others will not be as satisfactory. One distinct group usually refuses to accept the possibility of the impending disaster. They feel that it simply could not happen; or that if it does happen it will not be as severe as the authorities claim; or if it does happen and is as severe as the authorities claim, they will somehow be spared. These are persons who have usually never been through the type of disaster which has been forecast. They often present resistance toward preparedness or evacuation.

The reaction of another group is even less satisfactory. This group consists of those who would be helpless in any emergency situation, those who have previously gone through a disaster and suffered extensively as a result, or those who have little faith in governmental agencies as a protective force. This group may become involved in frantic overactivity, accomplishing little. During an evacuation they may be seen loading their cars with a variety of frivolous items, and then throwing them away as they select an item which they feel would be more practical to salvage. Such persons have been observed being evacuated while carrying a parakeet in a cage, and a green trading stamp book under their arm, yet complaining to the police that they wish to reenter the disaster area as they had left a variety of negotiable securities and important family records in the house. Persons who are involved in this overactive behavior are those who may well panic during a disaster, a topic which will be dealt with later.

Another negative reaction to warning seems to be a state of shock and disbelief, wherein a disaster victim becomes totally hopeless and lethargic intead of overactive. He may simply sit and stare at the activity going on about him and seems unable to respond in any way towards self-protection.

At the Time of Disaster

At the time of maximum occurrence of a disaster, those persons subject to its force usually are in some level of shock. Even those persons who have been subject to discipline and organization, such as public safety employees, will exhibit a degree of confusion and disoriented activity. During the actual occurrence of the disaster, there is almost an overwhelming tendency on the part of those in the area to watch its visible elements: be it a fire, tidal wave, or dam collapse. This period of shock, confusion, disorientation, or hypnosis is usually quite short for most persons. The actual occurrence of the disaster may, in some cases, have a settling and motivating effect on those persons whose activities and reactions were not considered satisfactory during the warning phase.

Immediately after Disaster

During this disaster control phase, most individuals who have been subject to the stress of the incident recover from their shock and exhibit a desire to help themselves and others. In many cases they seem to need some productive activity in order to reach psychological stabilization. They will exhibit suggestibility to directions and gratitude to disaster workers who permit them to help. Disaster victims who are organized and given objectives to accomplish must be closely and carefully supervised during this phase, as they are very liable to overexert themselves or collapse thus creating additional medical care problems. While their desire to help themselves is high, their productivity will probably be unsatisfactory. The disaster commander should be aware that in many disasters the largest number of disaster workers available are victims who are organized by public safety officers.

At the Time of Normalization

After disaster control has been achieved, the wounded cared for, the dead recovered and identified, the dangers eliminated, and the area safe for reentry, the psychology of returning disaster victims is usually characterized by a feeling of unity and brotherhood, appreciation to the governmental agencies for the work that they have done, gratefulness that the disaster was not worse, or that their lives were spared, and a desire to participate in plans and activities to restore the stricken community. The disaster commander should note, as well as all police administrators, that this is probably the best time for reports to be made to governmental legislative agencies and for requests to be made for equipment which was found to be needed during the disaster. City councils, county boards of supervisors, and state legislators are notorious for approving budgetary requests for disaster related equipment during this phase. It is also during this period that community support of the fire and police service will be at its height.

At the Time of Reflection

In the weeks and months that follow a major disaster, the mood of the victims may become quite negative. Feelings of cooperation with fellow disaster victims end and they are seen as competitors for such rehabilitative services as are available. Feelings of appreciation toward the governmental agencies disappear as victims see others whose property was less damaged or "better protected" and they begin to seek a scapegoat. Victims blame governmental agencies for the extent of their plight and closely question police, fire, and other public safety activities at the time of the disaster.

These negative relationships are heightened by the fact that during this period the disaster victim is usually placed on his own. Governmental and social services such as food, shelter, and medical treatment end and the victim is expected to fend for himself, rebuild his home, move to another area, and find another job if his place of employment was eliminated. Simultaneously he finds that the governmental loans which were expected to assist him in rebuilding his life are less than anticipated, the insurance company upon which he relied is either not going to reimburse his loss, or is going to do so at a much depreciated figure. It also is during this period that governmental legislative branches, reacting to the mood of the disaster victims, often conduct inquiries.

The disaster commander may find himself in the position of justifying his activities from the moment of disaster impact to the end of the control period. He may have to document his activities, justify his decisions, verify and rationalize his assignment of priorities, and in some extreme cases, defend himself against civil or criminal charges. It is at this time that a complete and accurate disaster log, supplemented by any other possible chronological records of disaster activities, becomes extremely valuable. The post-disaster recriminations have been so severe in a few incidents that the concerned law enforcement agencies have decided that in such future occurrences they will equip police officers with small portable battery operated tape recorders, and all contacts with citizens regarding evacuation, security or destruction of livestock, and abandonment of property will be recorded. In addition, many agencies who do not have recording capability in their communication center now plan to place a portable tape recorder by their radio transmitter so that they may document all communications during the disaster.

PANIC PROBLEMS

The topic of panic should be of extreme interest to police leaders as it has an unusual and distinct role in disasters. Panic, when it occurs during a disaster, cannot help but worsen the situation, result in higher loss of lives, or impede organization of victims toward survival. In some cases panic becomes the disaster itself; where a routine minor incident occurs and those in the vicinity create a panic mob, the panic crush itself becomes the disaster.

Panic Described

A panic mob occurs where a group of persons in some close proximity to each other are subject to a high degree of emotionalism, strain or fatigue, and then are presented with an immediate severe threat, or imagine that they are in such immediate danger. A few of the most unstable will then react by hysteria, seize a course of action, and execute some frantic activity toward that course of action which they believe will provide either relief or escape from the threatening danger. Other members of the group, although subject to the same emotional stresses and strain, rapidly lose their remaining stability in the face of the frantic activities of the first few crowd members to panic. The psychological aspects of imitation or the band wagon effect then takes place, and the balance of the individuals in the group follow the frantic first few. Thus, the entire group becomes a panic mob, intent on one course of action and blind to all other possible methods of escape.

The fact that they see no other alternative than the course of action that they are taking is probably the most important aspect in creating the final conditions which assure total panic mob behavior on the part of those present. The course of action selected by the first frantic few inevitably will not accommodate the mass of the group of people now seeking that method of escape. The exits are too few, the exit is too small, the life boat is not large enough, or there are not enough life boats. This phenomenon creates competition on the part of the panic mob to gain access to the escape device, and a crushing effect occurs at that point. Due to the trance-like state of panic mob activity, there is an inability to communicate by those at the escape device that it is nonexistent, too small, or defective. This causes an ever larger number of persons to press forward, thus crushing and smothering those who are trapped at the escape device.

Panic as a Part of a Disaster

Two examples may be cited; the first is the South Amboy Port explosion of May 19, 1950. In this instance, over 150 tons of military explosives detonated simultaneously and extensive damage resulted (see entire case study in Chapter 6). Residents in the vicinity, seeing a mushroom shaped cloud, felt that an atomic explosion had occurred. A number of panic mobs were created and these individuals fled out into the streets in an attempt to run away from expected radiation or other hazards. The explosion had scattered thousands of unexploded antipersonnel mines in the area. The panic mobs fleeing up the streets were endangering themselves by exposure to these antipersonnel mines. Some fifty mines were later recovered from the streets in the business and residential area.

A second example is the Indiana fairgrounds explosion of November 1, 1963. Several small panic mobs occurred in this disaster, some attempting to get across the ice to exits, others clogging the exits on the side where the explosions occurred (see case study in Chapter 6). Had the orchestra not continued to play following the explosions, it is estimated that severe panic crushes would have occurred.

Panic as a Disaster in Itself

This is the classic panic mob crush situation where some minor incident, which probably would not have caused material danger to most of those in the crowd, resulted in the creation of panic among a few which caused a panic mob to generate, creating a crushing situation that killed far more persons than the original incident could ever have threatened. Many examples exist. Probably the most graphic include the Iroquois theater fire in 1903 wherein over six hundred persons were killed primarily because of panic crush and smothering, the Triangle building fire in 1911 in which 146 persons were killed in two separate panic escape mobs, one group throwing themselves out of windows as an escape, the other packing a single fire exit; the Coconut Grove night club fire in 1942 in which 498 people died as a result of panic crushes against a few exits when a fire was discovered, and the Ringling Brothers Circus fire in 1944 in which 169 persons smothered to death in the escape chutes as a result of a panic crush mob when a fire occurred in the tent. In each of these cases the senseless frantic action of a panic mob created a set of circumstances which killed large numbers of persons who probably would have received little damage or injury from the original danger.

Panic Control

In either type of situation, panic as a part of a disaster or panic as a disaster in itself, there is a short period of time between the moment at which the threat or danger is perceived by the crowd, the moment the first few frantic members begin their senseless activities, and the time at which the balance of the crowd joins in the panic mob action. During these short intervals the panic crush mob may be averted if an authority figure can interrupt the chain of events. If some form of distraction can be achieved, so that the actions of the first few frantic individuals are ignored by the balance of those present, or if the authority figure can give a number of logical and reasonable alternate courses to that course of action taken by the first few, or if some sort of massive calming influence may be brought to bear, such as group singing, group activity participation, or if all these things can be accomplished along with a firm clarification which minimizes the nature of the hazard, then perhaps panic mob activity may be averted.

After the majority of those present enter into panic mob activity, control usually becomes futile and the only course of action left for authorities at the scene is to attempt to minimize the damage or loss of lives. These minimizing techniques depend on the situation, but occasionally it has been found effective by police officers, school teachers, and others to work at the edge of a panic mob, seizing individuals, and attempting to penetrate their hysteria by suggesting an alternative course of action. The use of physical barriers has been effective in some cases where one or two corridors or exits have become hopelessly jammed, and turnstiles or sliding chainlink fences may be used to direct persons toward other exits. Perhaps lights could be turned off in portions of the building where the panic crush is completely uncontrollable, thus directing others toward those exits, tunnels, or passageways which are lighted.

In any event, the message for policemen should be clear. He is an authority symbol because of his distinctive uniform and assigned role in society. The uniformed police officer who, in a calm manner, attempts to prevent or control panic will probably achieve some success. It is tragic that all too few police officers receive training in panic control and prevention.

Panic Prevention

Panic may best be prevented or controlled by providing meaningful participation for those in the crowd, by suggesting alternatives to the escape upon which they have fixed, and clarifying or discounting the nature of the threat. The prevention of the panic crushes at public events and large gatherings is a special topic which should receive some consideration. A survey of the case histories of many panic crushes shows they take place at stadiums, theaters, auditoriums, schools, and other locations during some special event. Inevitably these large gatherings are policed by the local law enforcement agency. It is quite common for a police department to assign numbers of officers to such events, either as a routine portion of their duties or as some sort of special paid duty.

It has been the author's observation that few agencies provide a specialized system for the policing of these events or provide training of any type for the officers working at them. It is blithely assumed that their presence will prevent panic or illegal activity, and that if a panic mob should occur, the officers through their standard training and expertise will know how to handle it.

A suggested system of policing public events includes a permit which is required of all persons responsible for presenting any event at which more than a given number of people will be assembled. This permit is not a revenue producing device, but requires the organizer to give complete information on the proposed event, including projections of attendance. The police department then determines the number of officers that should be assigned to the event for control purposes. Whether the cost of this extra policing is borne by the community or by the organization sponsoring the event is a matter for local determination.

The criteria for the decision regarding the number of policemen to be assigned include the type of event, the age level and type of participant, its location, and its time or duration. Obviously, an art show wherein two thousand people will observe two hundred paintings over an eight hour period in a mall requires less policing than a football game where fourteen thousand people will be assembled for three hours in a coliseum. The department will also determine the number of supervisors needed with respect to the number of policemen assigned, and the nature of the event.

The police department then designates a supervisor or a senior officer as the event officer.

The event officer contacts the promoter or organizers and views the scene of the event. He obtains or makes a map of the facility. He verifies on a checklist the type, location, and telephone number of all telephones in the facility. He verifies all exits and entrances, the type of lock, and any other obstacles which could prevent exit. He verifies location of the light switches and fuse box or panel control boxes for lighting and ventilation. He locates all firefighting equipment, verifies with the fire department or other public agency the maximum capacity for the facility. He determines the name and locations of the persons who will be present during the event who are in charge, who have special keys, or who have special knowledge of the building or facility.

The event officer, at a meeting just prior to the policing of the event, briefs all participating policemen on the general situation, their duties, the location of their assignments, and all other pertinent data. He hands them a series of maps of the facility, and a list of the telephones, fire equipment, and other data he has gathered. The event officer provides each officer working the assignment with a portable two-way radio.

One officer is assigned near the facilities office to assure that the building manager, janitor or others having control of the facility can be reached immediately to turn on or off ventilators, lights, open or unlock doors, and to assure that the police at the scene have rapid access to outside telephone communication. If an officer working the parking lights wants more illumination to prevent thefts, he merely contacts the inside officer who is assigned near the office by two-way portable radio. That officer contacts the building manager, and the correct light switch is thrown which illuminates the parking lot. Assume that a lady faints in a corridor. The nearest officer merely radios the policeman near the building manager's office to call for an ambulance to respond to a particular exit of the building. In this way, the officer can remain with the victim, yet the telephone request for an ambulance can be almost instantaneous.

The event officer continually tours the facility verifying that his policemen are on post and that they are aware of and executing their functions. If possible, the event officer secures portable public address units near a number of the fixed posts to which he has assigned officers so that if there is need to control a crowd by voice, it can be done more effectively. Through the adoption of these techniques in policing public events, it may be possible for a police department to prevent a panic mob from forming should an incident occur.

SUMMARY

Police administrators must understand the cycle of psychological moods which sweep a community subjected to disaster in order to maintain favorable community relations, maximize their effectiveness in dealing with the various legislative bodies, securing of favorable consideration in budget requests, and the timing of policy announcements. The disaster commander must be familiar with the motivation, psychological change, and behavior potential both of disaster victims and his own personnel to successfully control or direct them. Finally, policemen, police supervisors, and police managers must understand the origin and the control of panic mobs and be able to attempt to prevent such activity or control it should it occur, both at a disaster scene as well as in a routine event.

6
WHAT THE POLICE DISASTER COMMANDER SHOULD KNOW ABOUT COMMON DISASTERS

This chapter contains information on commonly occurring disasters and briefly describes their cause and damage effect. Police control problems and related hazards for each are discussed; and it is intended that this information provide a frame of reference for disaster response planning, and perhaps during an actual disaster, a ready source reference or action checklist.

AIRPLANE CRASHES

Cause

Airplane crashes are caused by a variety of circumstances: defective equipment, faulty judgment, weather complications, and occasionally explosions caused by intentional sabotage. Recently it would seem that many of the major airplane crashes are caused by mid-air collision and mechanical or communications failures while involved in taking off, landing, or maintaining flight patterns around major airports. Thus airplane crashes in highly populated and urban areas surrounding major air terminals have a high potential for future increase.

Damage Effect

Most airplane crashes involving commercial or large passenger craft result in total destruction of the airplane, and usually the death of all occupants. Most deaths are caused by impact injuries, but where fire occurs, the bodies are frequently burned beyond recognition. Mid-air collisions have the effect of scattering debris and victims over a wide area. Ground damage on impact is usually limited in area due to the single directional force of the airplane. Surface fatalities are usually high at the impact point, but victims on the perimeter of the impact are usually char-

Airplane crashes in populated areas can result in extensive loss of life. (Photo credit—Seattle Police Department.)

acterized by a high rate of minor and medium injuries caused by flying debris, glass and fire.

Related Hazards

Military aircraft involved in crashes may contain a variety of live munitions. The large quantity of highly inflammable fuel carried by commercial and military aircraft constitutes an extreme fire hazard, if not already ignited by the crash. The point of impact in urban areas is usually also characterized by downed telephone and high voltage electrical wires.

Predicted Frequency

The frequency of major airplane crashes, defined as those having twenty-five or more casualties, has been slightly more than four per year during the past decade. The locations of these disasters show an increasing tendency towards areas surrounding major air terminals. Prediction of future disasters is difficult because while increasing technological efforts toward flight safety will have a positive effect, increasing air traffic and greatly enlarged passenger capacity of aircrafts may alter the gains made through engineering.

Police Problems

One universal problem involved in airplane crashes is that of prompt notification. It is absolutely essential that the Civil Aeronautics Board and the Federal Aviation Agency be immediately notified of every airplane crash. Military authorities must be notified at once if military aircraft are involved. Generally, the Civil Aeronautics Board has primary authority in the investigation of civilian aircraft accidents involving death or an aircraft over 12,500 pounds in weight. The Federal Aviation Agency also investigates civilian aircraft accidents and will initiate prosecution should law violations be discovered.

As civilian or military authorities may be involved in investigating the aircraft crash, a major role of the police at the scene is protection of evidence. It is essential that a security perimeter be established at a reasonable distance around the impact area. The handling or disturbance of the aircraft or any parts must be avoided. In some cases, wreckage may be scattered a great distance from the primary impact area. This wreckage must be safeguarded and isolated prior to the investigation. Wreckage and debris should be disturbed only if necessary for life saving purposes, or to prevent further property damage. Investigating agencies will appreciate police cooperation by documenting the identity of witnesses to the crash, and by prompt photographing of the impact area, wreckage, and other related items.

Body recovery techniques should be somewhat modified with respect to air crash victims. If possible, bodies should be left as discovered until CAB or FAA investigators may view them. Where this is not possible, recovered bodies should be photographed as they are found in the wreckage and their position documented on a grid chart prior to removal. If the bodies are removed to a mortuary, it is imperative to advise coroners and morticians that no embalming procedures be done until approval is obtained from the investigating agencies. The coroner should further be requested not to release bodies to families without approval of the CAB or FAA.

Problems involved with passenger lists and the notification of next of kin make it imperative that the police not release names of victims at the scene. The press liaison officer should provide the press only with general information regarding the accident and should require the press to seek the exact aircraft flight number, name of airline, and other information from the commercial airline involved or from military authorities.

Military aircraft accidents present a slightly different problem in police control. Permission for the press to enter the disaster scene must be obtained from a military commander and while civilian police may not stop the press from taking photographs at the scene, they should advise reporters that it is a violation of federal law to photograph classified material, and officers should notify the military authorities as soon as possible which photographers were taking pictures at the scene.

AVALANCHES AND LAND SLIDES

Cause

Avalanches are caused when large masses of snow, rock, or earth slide from a higher elevation to a lower level. Avalanches may be caused by a variety of factors including earthquakes, floods which cause mudslides, build-ups of snow or ice in mountain areas, and the activities of construction workers in building roads, dams, and firebreaks.

Damage Effect

Buildings and vehicles are usually covered with the sliding debris, mud, snow, or dirt. Victims are usually killed, survivors are few. Death results from crushing and smothering. In past avalanches most victims were either killed outright, or were virtually unharmed.

Related Hazards

Avalanches almost always destroy water, sewage, and other utility systems. Ruptured gas lines increase possibilities of fire during rescue operations.

Predicted Frequency

While minor avalanches and earth slides are quite common, particularly in and around construction sites, major tragedies of this nature where fifty or more victims are killed, occur at a rate of less than one per year throughout the world. They occur more frequently in steep or mountainous areas, or in hilly areas during heavy rain fall.

Police Problems

Immediate rescue is vital due to the smothering effect of the avalanche. The application of techniques involving rescue from debris becomes essential by first officers at the scene. Conducting rescue intelligence on the number and location of other probable

Avalanches and landslides in populated mountain or seaside cliff areas can cause complicated body recovery problems. (Photo credit—South Bay Daily Breeze, Torrance, California.)

survivors is essential. Convergence control is also essential to prevent unauthorized individuals from creating additional avalanches which will endanger rescue workers or further worsen the situation.

Rescue workers should attempt to initiate a tap and listen system to locate live survivors. In some avalanche tragedies, victims have been trapped in voids and have been able to live until their supply of oxygen was exhausted. If these victims can be located and an airway can be driven through to them, they may later be rescued.

Most avalanche scenes are in rural areas, and the arrival time for significant numbers of police or other public safety officers is necessarily long. The first officer at the scene of an avalanche may find himself responsible for the disaster response activities of those present at the location for some length of time.

BLIZZARDS

Cause

A blizzard is an extremely severe snow storm which combines strong winds, drifting, blinding snow, temperatures which may reach twenty to thirty degrees below zero, coupled with winds of from fifty to sixty miles an hour. Blinding snow is driven with such great force that deep drifts accumulate and visibility is sharply reduced. Blizzards usually occur when cold, polar air comes in contact with low pressure disturbances.

Damage Effect

The blinding, drifting snow will close roads to vehicle traffic by banking huge drifts across open areas. The drifting effect of the snow will occasionally cover entire buildings. In some cases, rows of automobiles parked on a highway may be covered with drifts from six to eight feet deep. Persons who attempt to walk in blizzards are frequently blinded and feel that they are suffocating. Electrical wires are frequently brought down by the weight of the snow.

Sudden blizzards often trap motorists in their automobiles until snow plows can reach them. (Photo credit—California Highway Patrol.)

Related Hazards

A major blizzard will paralyze all highway traffic and may reduce telephone communications or electrical power due to wires being broken down by the heavy snow. People are trapped whereever they may be when the blizzard strikes. Children will be trapped in schools or on stalled school buses. Workers must remain in the factory or office, persons at home may have to spend one to five days with such provisions as they may have in the house. Persons who go outside in an attempt to walk for help are frequently overcome by the force of the storm and frozen to death.

Due to the extreme cold, persons who are confined within homes and other buildings frequently burn gas and oil heaters without adequate ventilation, thus reducing the oxygen available and occasionally causing suffocation. Motorists on a highway frequently roll up all windows and run their engines to keep the automobile heater going as they wait for snow plow or rescue. Exhaust leaks in the vehicles occasionally permit carbon monoxide to asphyxiate these motorists.

Predicted Frequency

Conditions favorable to the occurrence of blizzards can be forecast quite accurately, but the condition develops so quickly that warnings seem never to occur sufficiently in advance of the arrival of the storm. Blizzards occur in the United States each winter, and are generally formed in the Rocky Mountains and plains states. The states of North Dakota, South Dakota, Minnesota, Wisconsin, Iowa, Nebraska, eastern Montana, and eastern Wyoming are most susceptible to severe blizzards, although they may occur anywhere within the middle west, and occasionally as far south as Texas.

Police Problems

The police are as immobilized by a blizzard as is the general public. It becomes almost impossible to maintain any type of patrol activity. Because the American public is now well equipped

with transistorized miniature radios, the police may involve themselves in a public safety warning program during a blizzard. Police may contact local radio and television stations to provide structured public service messages warning the public on the hazards of the blizzard. The public should be warned or advised:
1. Not to go out in the blizzard. To remain where they are.
2. If they must go out in the storm, techniques of tying rope or wire together in such a way that they can find their way back to the door if they are unable to make it to the next structure.
3. On proper ventilation of heating equipment in buildings to prevent suffocation.
4. On how to survive when trapped in an automobile, including ventilation and heating information.
5. Information to reassure parents of children who are trapped in schools and others who are separated from their families to prevent panic and to lower anxiety.

At the police station an information and registry service is often conducted so that persons may leave their names and the location where they have found shelter so that persons inquiring after their safety may be reassured, or so that they can be contacted if their skills are needed during the blizzard.

CHEMICAL-NUCLEAR ACCIDENTS

Cause

Chemical or nuclear materials which are hazardous are today stored in almost every community in America. In addition, they are frequently transported by truck or rail, and in some cases, pipelines. Accidents are caused by a rupture of a transportation or storage device causing the hazardous material to endanger the lives of those within its range. These accidents may occur separately, as with a traffic accident or a minor explosion in a plant, or they may be connected with another disaster which caused severe rupturing of vessels and containers. Earthquakes, floods, and fires may cause, as a secondary effect, the leakage of hazardous materials.

Radiation detection, following accidents which cause nuclear materials to pollute an area, is a primary disaster control technique. (Photo credit—Honolulu Police Department.)

Damage Effect

The damage created by the accident varies with the type of material which is released. Poisonous dusts, fumes, mists, vapors, and gases from chemicals or pesticides may kill any person who is exposed to them for varying periods of time. In addition, they may contaminate an area which may not be reentered for a considerable period of time and may require extensive clean-up. Radioactive materials may create radiation sickness in victims and may also contaminate areas for long periods of time. Other material such as rocket fuel or corrosive chemicals may also be explosive in addition to being toxic.

Related Hazards

In addition to the hazards of poisoning, fire, and explosion, chemical and nuclear accidents create a high panic potential.

Predicted Frequency

This type of disaster is too recent in our society for any reliable statistics to have been developed. The potential is greatest in industrial areas where hazardous chemicals are extensively used and in those agricultural areas where extremely toxic poisons or inflammable-explosive chemical fertilizers are stored.

Police Problems

One primary police problem in controlling this type disaster is recognition of the substance involved. Extensive training should be undertaken with the patrol and traffic segments of the police service on the subject of identification of hazardous materials. Most vehicles containing such materials are plainly marked. Police must be trained to interrogate drivers of commercial vehicles at accident scenes regarding the nature of the cargo and potential hazard. They must be trained to examine bills of lading or manifest carried in the vehicles in an attempt to learn the nature of leaking hazardous materials. In addition, they must be trained to identify the various markings used to identify hazardous and dangerous materials.

At the scene of an accident where the police have reason to believe that there is a leakage of a hazardous chemical or radioactive substance, they must immediately conduct an evacuation of those in danger, with primary attention being given to potential victims who are downwind of the leak or accident. Immediately following this, the surrounding area should be evacuated in case of a shift in wind direction. The area should be cordoned as completely as possible to prevent reentry of persons into a hazardous area. Proper authorities, depending on the nature of the incident, should be contacted at once: the public health officer, the poison control center, and the local civil defense office. Information should be obtained from these authorities regarding on-scene decontamination and proper protective or respiratory devices to be used.

Following this notification or contact, the next steps will be at the direction of the proper authority most knowledgeable regarding the incident. The police should locate all persons who may have been contaminated and insure that they receive proper decontamination treatment. They should also insure that their own personnel and others at the scene are wearing the proper protective masks or are using the specified safety equipment. Where individuals are overcome by toxic effects the police must provide rapid ambulance transportation in such a manner as not to further increase the tendency to panic, and must alert hospitals as to the type of problem and number of victims they may expect.

DAM AND RESERVOIR COLLAPSES

Cause

Large bodies of water contained in reservoirs or backed up behind dams create tremendous pressures on the structure. If the retaining earth or structure is damaged by an earthquake or explosion, or is structurally or geologically weak, or if the pressure of the retained water is rapidly increased due to flooding or a landslide, small leaks in the retaining matter will occur. Almost all dam collapses, and the resulting releases of large amounts of water, start as small leaks which through rapid erosion and high pressure enlarge until total collapse occurs.

Damage Effect

Damage from dam collapses vary depending upon the height of the dam above the surrounding surfaces and the amount of water contained. Dams at some altitude create a high velocity water flow when they burst which causes extensive structural damage in the affected low-lying areas, sweeping everything in its path. Low level dams or reservoirs merely flood surrounding areas when they collapse, and structural damage is minor, except

Dam and reservoir collapses often occur following earthquakes. (Photo credit—Ralph L. Emerson.)

for that which is caused by flooding and submersion. Loss of life is due primarily to drowning.

Related Hazards

Those hazards commonly connected with flooding are applicable to dam collapses and they include the possibility of fires, electrical shorting, contamination of water, sewage overflow, and occasionally the release or mixture of toxic, corrosive or explosive chemicals. In addition, rural, western, and southern areas subject to flooding by dam collapse have experienced displacement of poisonous snake or rodent populations which create hazards in nearby dry areas.

Predicted Frequency

Throughout the world there has been only approximately one dam collapse per year, most of which have been relatively minor as far as loss of life is concerned. Yet one incident in Brazil during 1960 claimed over one thousand victims and another in 1963 which occurred in Italy claimed over three thousand victims. Their frequency is closely tied to the occurrence of earthquakes, landslides, and avalanches.

Police Problems

Primary police problems in this type of disaster are warning and evacuation. Given sufficient warning, and an effective evacuation system, most fatalities due to dam collapses could be eliminated. Following attempts to warn and evacuate, police responsibility includes a cordon of possibly affected low-lying areas to prevent reentry, and during later stages of the disaster, conducting rescue operations, body recovery and identification, and prevention of looting. Many western and southern law enforcement agencies issue small caliber shot shells to their officers following incidents of flooding as they are frequently called upon to destroy snakes, rodents, and other animals which may present a hazard in nearby living areas.

EARTHQUAKES

Cause

It is believed that earthquakes are caused by a gradual change in the distribution of pressure or weight in the earth's crust; stress developed by such changes causes sudden fractures or slips along a preexisting fault, which results in a shock wave, traveling outward along the earth's surface at speeds of several miles per second.

Damage Effect

The effect of earthquake shock waves will cause collapse of structures including buildings, bridges, and dams. Most deaths and injuries are created from these collapsing structures, crushed by falling debris, or struck by shattered glass.

Related Hazards

Earthquakes create a large number of related hazards. The shock waves or tremors will cause breaks in electrical wires, leaks in gas mains, ruptures of tanks holding all varieties of explosive and flammable or toxic chemicals, building and dam collapses, flooding from tidal waves, landslides or avalanches, traffic accidents caused by collapsed roadways and bridges, and fires created by escaping gas and downed powerlines.

Predicted Frequency

Over seven hundred earthquake shocks per year are recorded which are strong enough to cause damage. Most of these originate beneath the sea, however, and their effects are not felt. In the United States, well over two-thirds of all earthquake activity occurs in Pacific Coast States. In the interior western portion of the United States there is a small earthquake zone whose activity extends from Montana southward into northern Arizona.

Numerous earthquakes have occurred during the past history of the United States on the Eastern seaboard and in the Mississippi River basin. Twelve major earthquakes with fatality rates

Collapse of buildings during an earthquake is probably the greatest cause of death and injury. (Photo credit—Ralph L. Emerson.)

of fifty or more have occurred during the past decade, indicating that throughout the world we can expect approximately one major earthquake per year.

Police Problems

Immediately following an earthquake the police facility itself should be rapidly inspected to prevent fires, to insure that the communication center is intact, that auxiliary generators are functioning if needed, and that lights and communications within the building will permit it to be used as a temporary headquarters. Following this, patrol units and all available personnel should be used to scout collapsed buildings in the areas most severely damaged in an attempt to put into operation the four-stage debris rescue plan. This plan should be implemented in cooperation with other responding public safety agencies.

Patrol forces should also scout the entire area to determine if any fires have started. Early fire warning is extremely important immediately following an earthquake. Many fires are started by broken electrical wires, escaping gas, spilled fuel, and other inflammables from storages containers. The situation is greatly worsened by the fact that many water mains are ruptured thus making fire fighting a highly difficult task. Citizens experience difficulty in reporting fires immediately after an earthquake because telephone communications are usually disrupted, or so many individuals are calling the fire and police station that the switchboards become overloaded.

Following rescue duties and fire scouting, patrol forces should attempt to locate and evacuate those buildings that have obviously been weakened by the quake and which may be collapsed by after-shocks. In addition, they should attempt to identify those walls, chimneys, and other structures, usually of brick or stone, which appear to be unstable and cordon them off should an after-shock cause them to fall.

A higher injury rate may be expected in earthquakes than in most other disasters, and as entire geographic areas are affected, there is a probability that hospitals may be destroyed or become

What the Police Disaster Commander Should Know

unusable just as schools, residences, and businesses. For this reason it is advisable to establish a victim transportation system to distant or unaffected hospitals. Because of the extreme communications problems caused by earthquakes, the police service may have to arrange for and dispatch such long distance victim transportation through their own radio system.

An additional problem occurs in obtaining manpower to cope with the emergency. Earthquakes tend to be area-wide, affecting entire counties or multiple county areas, and it may be extremely difficult to obtain mutual aid. During an earthquake, a police disaster commander can best count on manpower from his own department, men called up from an off-duty status, reserves, and volunteers from his own community.

Two measurements of earthquakes are important: magnitude and intensity. Magnitude will be measured by scientists on the Richter Scale. Intensity may be measured on the Mercalli Intensity Scale, and may be of value to the press liaison officer. The intensity scale is based on a I to XII range and uses roman numerals in order to further distinguish it from the magnitude scale which uses arabic numbers.

I. Shaking not strong enough to be noticed.
II. Shaking barely felt by few people. Birds and animals are disturbed.
III. Shaking felt indoors. Vibrations similar to passing of lightly loaded truck. May not be recognized as an earthquake.
IV. Shaking felt indoors by many people. Dishes, windows, and doors rattle. Wakens a few light sleepers. Vibration like passing of heavily loaded truck. Hanging objects swing.
V. Felt indoors by everyone—outdoors by most people. Slight excitement. Dishes, glassware, and windows break in some cases. Vases and unstable objects overturn and many fall. Hanging objects and doors swing generally. Pictures knock against wall. Furniture might move to slight extent.

VI. Frightening. Awakens all sleepers and frightens many people. Liquids set in strong motion. Trees and bushes shake. Poorly constructed buildings may be damaged. Plaster falls in small amounts. Dishes, glasses and windows break. Furniture may overturn. Heavy furniture moves.

VII. Frightens everyone. General alarm. Everyone runs outdoors. Difficult to stand. People driving cars notice shaking. Damage negligible to buildings of good design. Poorly built buildings damaged. Plaster and stucco fall. Windows and some furniture break. Weak chimneys break at roof line. Bricks and stones dislodge.

VIII. People hysterical. People driving cars disturbed. Trees break off. Damage slight in brick structures built to withstand earthquakes. Damage considerable to other buildings and some collapse. Solid stone walls crash and break. Chimneys, columns and monuments twist and fall. Heavy furniture moves tremendously or overturns.

IX. Panic. Ground cracks. Considerable damage to earthquake-proof structures, great in others and some collapse. Some shift off foundations. Some damage to underground pipes.

X. Panic. Fissures appear in ground. Landslides. Dangerous cracks appear in retaining walls. Railroad rails bend. Most buildings and their foundations destroyed. Open cracks and wavy folds open in street pavement. Very destructive.

XI. Panic. Damage severe to dams, dikes, and embankments. Few, if any, masonry, buildings remain standing. Bridges are wrecked. Buried pipe lines completely out of service. Railroad rails bend and tilt.

XII. Panic. Damage is total. Fault slips develop in firm rock. Objects thrown upward into air. Violent shaking.

The scale may be useful in police communications and in contacts with the public following an earthquake, and prior to the time that an official magnitude has been determined for the earthquake.

ELECTRICITY OR TELEPHONE BLACKOUT

Cause

Electrical telephone service may be cut off for communities, cities, or even entire portions of a state, when electrical generating centers or telephone communication centers are paralyzed by an overload, suffer mechanical difficulties, are destroyed by fire, or occasionally when paralyzed by sabotage. Recent experiences have ranged in type and scope but good examples along the Eastern seaboard during the summer have occurred where large metropolitan centers have been without electricity for two or three days.

Damage Effect

Loss of lighting at night always increases the potential for vandalism, looting, and thievery. With the loss of telephone communications, whereby citizens may report crimes or request help, the criminal potential is extensive. Additional hazards involve routine calls for assistance including medical, fire, and utility which cannot be completed due to electrical or communications failures.

Related Hazards

Traffic congestion from nonfunctioning signals and fires started by candles may be expected.

Predicted Frequency

Such disasters have been infrequent in our past history, but there is every indication that they will multiply in the future, due to increased population, maximum utilization of electrical and communications equipment and appliances, competition between ecological interests and power generating facilities, increasing dependence upon automation and a decreasing quality of public utility employees.

Police Problems

When an electrical or telephone blackout occurs, the police must respond by maximizing community patrol to cope with possible increased criminal activities. Communications are at the heart of the problem. Almost every family possesses a battery operated transistor radio. If a commercial radio station can be put back into operation through some auxiliary power source, public service messages can be broadcast over this frequency. The police service, in cooperation with the fire service, should set up communication centers in every geographic area. These may be the local fire station or an intersection where a patrol car may be parked, or possibly an intersection where a police reserve unit with a citizens band radio may be parked. Citizens should be advised continually by public service messages of the location of these communication centers. Citizens should be further advised that they should proceed at once to the given intersection or fire station in their area when assistance is needed. As the citizens respond to these locations, their needs may be broadcast through the police radio, citizens band radio, or fire department radio and a proper response may be made to their needs.

EPIDEMICS

Cause

Epidemics are caused by infectious microorganisms or viruses of a highly communicable nature, usually coupled with a lack of resistance on the part of the victims or inability to develop an immunity to the virus. Epidemics are made much worse where people live in highly congested areas or where there is poor sanitation, undernourishment, and inadequate health standards. In the future, epidemics may be caused by viruses or organisms which are created by man through his ecological imbalance or those which are returned to earth from outer space.

Damage Effect

Primary damage is created by the disease killing victims, usually by the thousands.

Related Hazards

A variety of problems are created during an epidemic over and above the sickness and death of the diseased victims. In some areas there may be a number of instances of panic in which large numbers of the population attempt to flee from a stricken area. In the past, the area from which a significant population has fled to avoid an epidemic has been characterized by fires and looting. Riots occur, particularly where there is a scarcity of food, medical attention, or other services. Crime increases have been noted on the part of that portion of the population who feel that they have become infected and will probably die anyway. Almost all community services break down during an epidemic as few people report for work because they fear traveling on public transportation or mingling with co-workers. Telephone and utilities services usually become overtaxed and break down.

Predicted Frequency

Epidemics are erratic and unpredictable. Until 1920, we experienced at least one disastrous epidemic every generation. Recent history has shown a reduction in epidemics due to advancements in medical science, public health, and sanitation. However, the trend in our society is toward a larger population living in more closely compacted areas, and a new strain or virus could cause a worse epidemic than previously experienced.

Police Problems

The onset of an epidemic is gradual, and the police response will be well integrated with public health and other community agencies. One primary problem is that police ranks will be disseminated by the epidemic as much or more than other organizations. This is due to the constant community contact the police must maintain. During the epidemic there will be a constant problem of lack of adequate manpower, thus reserves and volunteer police must be recruited and utilized extensively. In addition, if community quarantine sectors are established, the police must decentralize their operation to the extent that their personnel will remain within the quarantine sector. This tends to decrease flexibility, places additional manpower requirements on the department, and will create communications and logistical problems. The same communications problem as described under electrical and telephone blackouts will occur as large numbers of utility workers will fail to report for duty. Primary police duties will be to attempt to maintain community communication services of an emergency nature, prevention of panics, and the prevention or control of riots which occur. In addition, the police may be required to maintain the quarantine sectors, enforce curfews, and prevent citizens from moving from one part of the community to another.

EXPLOSIONS

Cause

Explosions are caused by a release of energy created when gases rapidly expand. The expansion of these gases may be caused by the rapid burning of some substance or fuel which overheats the gases or by a spontaneous combustion of several chemicals coming in contact, which immediately create a rapidly expanding volume of gas.

Damage Effect

Persons near the explosion are either killed or injured from the blast and concussion. Persons further away are frequently injured by debris or fragments propelled by the explosion. Buildings and other structures often collapse. This causes a separate group of casualties who are injured in the collapse of the structure. Injuries are reduced as the distance outward from the force of the explosion increases, but in some instances victims have been seriously injured from shattered windows many thousands of feet from the source of the explosion.

Related Hazards

The possibility of fire is a continual hazard following an explosion. Ruptured gas pipes, electrical shorts, and electrical wires which have been disconnected all constitute a high fire hazard.

Explosions, particularly in industrial areas, may cause secondary disasters including escaping hazardous chemicals and fire. (Photo credit—South Bay Daily Breeze, Torrance, California.)

The explosion itself is, of course, a strong ignition source. In many instances, crowds which have responded to the scene of the explosion have been injured by subsequent explosions.

Predicted Frequency

Most of the major explosions with extremely high death rates have been caused by detonating munitions or fuel during war time. However, smaller explosions occur frequently throughout the world and these are usually related to the manufacturing, storage or transportation of a variety of chemicals or materials.

Police Problems

Following a major explosion, police and fire personnel on the scene will be faced with a rubble or debris rescue problem. Explosions tend to draw large crowds of people, and they must be kept behind a perimeter at a distance which will protect them should a second explosion occur. This makes crowd control an important police priority. Coordinating ambulance and hospital activities is also of great importance following an explosion as this type disaster tends to generate more persons with minor and medium severity injuries than almost any other type of disaster.

During the latter stage of the disaster control operation, the police will undoubtedly be involved in body recovery and identification. Recent social conditions create a possibility that explosions may be acts of sabotage, which somewhat complicates disaster control because of the criminal investigation aspect. In some recent instances, panic has occurred in nearby similar buildings or industries following an explosion. In these cases, workers repeated rumors that the explosion was an act of sabotage and that similar bombs were planted in their buildings. Thus, rumor and panic control may also be police problems following an explosion.

FIRES

Cause

A fire is really a chemical process in which some fuel is raised to ignition temperature and combines rapidly with oxygen or

Fires, either rural or urban, have disaster potential when control is lost due to wind and climatic conditions. (Photo credit—Ralph L. Emerson.)

some other combustion supporter which produces large amounts of heat. Fires can occur anywhere that a suitable fuel exists. In urban areas, they most frequently involve structures or industrial areas. In rural areas forest and brush fires are most common. The combustible materials are ignited by a variety of sources, but those most frequently identified are electrical accidents, smoking and matches, faulty equipment including heaters and stoves, spontaneous ignition, acts of nature such as lightning, and other accidents which include airplane crashes and explosions.

Damage Effect

Fires destroy extensive property and render most structures unusable for varying periods of time. Most persons who are killed or injured are victims of inhalation of toxic smoke rather than actually being burned. Fires frequently cause the collapse of buildings which trap victims or which complicates their escape, thus causing panic.

Related Hazards

Panic may occur in congested areas where a major fire occurs unless adequate fire drills or pre-fire conditioning has occurred. Many injuries are caused by victims attempting to escape the flames. In so doing, they often throw themselves from window ledges, leap through plate glass windows, and otherwise involve themselves in secondary types of injuries.

Predicted Frequency

Fires resulting in deaths occur daily in the United States. Although over ten thousand persons a year are killed by fires, most fatal fires kill only one or two victims. By far the highest death rate occurs when a structure in an urban area is involved: hotels, schools, factories, or entertainment centers. Highest fatality rates seem to center in school and theater fires. Although extensive safety inspections have occurred in recent years, over twenty-one hundred school fires per year are still reported in this country.

Police Problems

One police problem which occurs in many fire situations is that of proper notification of fire departments. Many tragedies have been worsened by the assumption by the first police officers on the scene that the fire department has been called. It should be well established in all patrol procedures that the first unit at the scene of a fire will immediately make a radio or telephone report to the police dispatcher of the location and nature of the fire. It is far better for the fire department to have too many notifications of a fire than for everyone to assume that someone else has called the fire department and have them arrive fifteen to thirty minutes late.

Evacuation is usually a police problem with a major fire. Individuals in neighborhoods which may fall in the path of the fire must be removed. In addition, the police service must provide a cordon around the fire to keep crowds of sightseers from interfering with fire department personnel and to prevent them from being injured by falling buildings or a rapid change of fire direction.

Although most victims who are killed in a fire die of inhalation of toxic fumes, if there are a large number of persons injured by burning, it will create special problems in hospital transportation. Burn victims require extensive and special treatment. The capacity of most hospitals is quickly filled with the first few victims and there develops a need to transport burn victims directly to hospitals some distance from the scene. This may or may not become a police transportation problem, depending upon supply of ambulances, and the degree to which local medical services are organized to meet disaster.

Fires in rural areas usually have a much lower death and injury rate. One special police problem which occurs in forest and brush fires is that of destruction of livestock. The policy should be clear in rural law enforcement agencies as to authority of the officer to destroy burned and injured livestock, with or without owner's permission. Post-disaster legal ramifications have created some unpleasant circumstances with regard to this activity.

FLOODS

Cause

Floods in sea coast areas are usually caused by ocean disturbances, such as hurricanes or tidal waves. Inland floods are usually caused by sustained rainfall or the too rapid melting of snow in the mountains although they are occasionally caused by dam collapse.

Damage Effect

Rapid flooding destroys structures, and, depending upon the velocity of the water, may wash away everything in its path. Slow flooding will merely cause a rise in the water level and most structures will not collapse. In any event, the major cause of death is drowning and there are usually few injuries.

Related Hazards

One related hazard, which is not usually considered, is that of fire. Fires commonly occur during flooding, and are caused by electrical shorting and the mixture of chemicals through flooding of industrial or storage areas. Occasionally storage tanks which contain fuel and other chemicals are ruptured by the pressure of the flood, and the inflammable fluids are floated to the surface and ignited. Additional related hazards have to do with the contamination of water and food during the later stages of the flood.

Predicted Frequency

Inland floods are predictable; each year an average of 75,000 Americans are driven from their homes and an average of eighty people per year are killed by drowning. Coastal floods are sporadic and are related to the occurrence of hurricanes or earthquakes.

Police Problems

Evacuation is a major police problem during a flood because it is difficult to convince victims that they should leave their

Floods may be of sudden onset following a dam burst, or gradual onset following heavy rain or rapid snow thaw. (Photo credit—Bee Newspaper, Modesto, California.)

property. The gradual onset of a flood deludes many that it will stop short of reaching their property. Occasionally it has been necessary to arrest and transport flood victims from a dangerous area during an evacuation. Following the onset of a flood, the police may be required to participate in rescue by boat and helicopter, and in addition, station officers along waterways to attempt to observe victims clinging to debris and being carried downstream. The slow onset usually relieves police service from maintaining the evacuation center as there is sufficient time for the Red Cross or other public service agency to assume this role. In southern and western areas the police have been plagued by calls from residents whose property has been invaded by snakes and rodents who are fleeing the high waters.

HURRICANES

Cause

The cause of hurricanes is not completely known. A hurricane is a storm which is circular or rotary in nature, developing winds over seventy miles per hour. It moves at a rate of from ten to fifteen miles per hour in a given direction, and it may be a hundred or more miles wide.

Damage Effect

Hurricanes cause very heavy rainstorms which result in rapidly rising water levels. The very high winds created by a hurricane develop high tides which may be fifteen feet over normal. The combination of the heavy rains and high tides cause extreme coastal lowland flooding. The combination of high waves and winds tend to smash buildings, bridges, and other structures. Most deaths are from drowning.

Related Hazards

Hazards usually following floods, such as fire and contamination, follow the occurrence of a hurricane.

Predicted Frequency

Yearly several hurricanes occur in the Atlantic, usually in August, September or October. Occasionally, similar storms occur in the Pacific where they are called typhoons. The Eastern seacoast can expect to be struck by a serious hurricane at least once every two years. Pacific typhoons are less predictable in frequency.

Police Problems

Ample hurricane warning is provided and it is usually possible to plot the location where it will create the most damage. Adequate time is available for the police to plan manpower requirements and to conduct proper evacuation of low-lying areas. Following the hurricane police problems relate primarily to rescue of those who evaded the evacuation and the cordoning of the stricken area to prevent reentry until public health officials have declared it to be safe. Patrols to prevent looting are occasionally necessary. In addition the police may have to establish emergency communication systems for the public as both electrical power and the telephone system are usually disrupted.

POLLUTION ALERTS

Cause

Pollutants in the air or water reach such a stage that an extreme health menace occurs. This may be air pollution, auto exhaust, or industry caused carbon monoxide, or it could be a DDT or mercury level increase in the water or food supply.

Damage Effect

It can be expected that the communications systems of the public safety and the public health service would be flooded with inquiries for information and with calls for ambulance service. Many victims whose previous medical history lowered their resistance to the particular pollution involved would be stricken. In addition there would be many new victims overcome by the particular nature of the new pollutant. In addition, it is forecast that there might be localized panic.

Related Hazards

It is estimated that the related hazards to a major pollution alert would be similar to those suffered by an epidemic.

Predicted Frequency

This is unknown as no community has ever suffered a major pollution alert to the extent that it was declared a disaster. However Los Angeles, New York, and Birmingham have been very close to such an emergency, and the potential throughout the country seems to be on the increase.

Police Problems

The police problems of a pollution alert are unknown, as such a disaster has never occurred. We can assume that there may be panic riots and the possibility is always present that communication and utilities workers may not be able to report, causing many of the problems described under epidemics. The appendix contains a description of the Los Angeles County air pollution alert system. (See Appendix J, Chap. 8).

TORNADOES

Cause

Tornadoes, also called twisters or cyclones, are believed to be caused when several masses of air meet from different directions, usually along a weather front. A rotary storm of great height is created. The storm is usually accompanied by heavy rains and winds of a velocity which may range from two hundred to four hundred miles per hour. A vertical funnel is usually visible. The storm base on ground surface can be as small as a few feet or as much as a mile in diameter. The storm funnel moves at an average speed of from thirty-five to forty miles per hour, and the average tornado cuts a path sixteen miles in length.

Torndoes smash buildings and make missiles of light rubble.

Damage Effect

Buildings are crushed by the tremendous air pressure and the vacuum which is created. Almost everything which has been torn loose or which is light enough for the winds to move becomes a missile. People who are caught away from protection are lifted in the air and often smashed into objects. Tornadoes kill an average of two hundred twenty-two Americans per year, and injure well over two thousand others.

Related Hazards

Fires often occur following tornadoes. Gas lines are frequently broken and fuel containers are ruptured. Electrical wires are broken and although there may have been a heavy downpour of rain during the brief tornado, it is not unusual for numerous fires to be started. An additional related hazard is the possible occurrence of a second tornado following the first within thirty to forty minutes.

Predicted Frequency

Tornadoes are a peculiarly American disaster, seeming to rarely occur on other continents. Hundreds occur in the United States each year, most occurring from February to July, usually in the afternoon hours. Although tornadoes occur nationwide, they are most common in the southern midwest from the Rockies to the Mississippi, and from Kansas and Iowa on the north.

Police Problems

Tornadoes give little warning and evacuation in their path is rarely possible. Police buildings, vehicles, and personnel are as susceptible to tornado damage as are others in the community. On any warning of a tornado, all police personnel and units should be advised to seek shelter until the danger passes. Personnel should attempt to get under ground or inside secure buildings, keeping well away from windows.

Immediately after the tornado has passed, police patrols should attempt to locate the areas of damage, report fires, and begin rescue work in collapsed buildings. While many victims will be found inside the rubble of crushed buildings, searchers should be aware that persons who are caught outside during a tornado may be found in a variety of unusual locations due to the extremely high winds and lifting effect of the tornado. The police should insure that electricity in the area struck by the tornado is turned off as soon as possible to prevent fires.

Although it is impossible to prevent the formation of crowds, the police must cordon the perimeter of damaged areas to prevent looting and other activities. On several occasions, a second tornado has occurred following the first, and caught large numbers of spectators in the open. Tornadoes create large numbers of injured, and hospital or ambulance facilities will be extremely taxed. Unfortunately, victims of tornadoes are rarely grouped to permit the development of ambulance dispatch posts, thus the police at the scene must, through their own communication system, attempt to assure full ambulance loads leaving the area.

TIDAL WAVES

Cause

Tidal waves are generated by sub-marine earthquakes which create a sea wave, a pressure wave or a series of such waves. These tidal waves travel at speeds of approximately four hundred miles per hour, and may go as far as eight thousand miles. They may be only a few feet high in the open sea, but when the tidal wave arrives in shallow water it slows in velocity and the height of the wave increases. Some have been over fifty feet in height when they struck the shore. It is often characteristic of a tidal wave that there will be a drop in the water level on the shore line just prior to the arrival of the wave.

Damage Effect

The tidal wave rushes onto the shore with great force, battering buildings and structures which are well above normal tide levels. As the wave sweeps on over the shore line, it causes extensive flooding, particularly at the mouths of rivers. The wave

Tidal waves, caused by earthquakes, often sweep through the path of least resistance as this aerial view of Seward, Alaska, indicates. (Photo credit—U. S. Army.)

may even run upstream some distance. Most deaths are caused by drowning or by crushing from debris.

Related Hazards

Multiple waves often occur and in several disasters people have returned to flooded areas to be caught by the next wave. Other related hazards are similar to those encountered with flooding or hurricanes.

Predicted Frequency

As they are tied to earthquakes, major tidal waves may be expected to occur every few years. They are most common along the coasts of the Pacific and Indian Oceans, but it is conceivable that a tidal wave could occur along the shoreline of any ocean or any major lakes if affected by earthquake activity.

Police Problems

In the United States, particularly along the West Coast, tidal wave warnings usually occur with sufficient time to permit evacuation. The "Seismic Sea-Wave Warning System" is a cooperative effort involving seismograph stations, tidal stations, governmental and private communication services, and a variety of experts from the public and private organizations. The Coast and Geodetic Survey unit of the United States Department of Commerce accepts responsibility for administering and operating a warning in the Pacific Ocean area. Operational control of the warning system is maintained by the Honolulu Observatory of the Coast and Geodetic Survey. The Honolulu Observatory initiates the warning message through the Federal Aviation Agency or through a military services communication system. The National Air Raid Warning System is used to transmit warnings on a statewide basis to concerned areas within the United States. In California, the State Disaster Office receives its warning from the National Warning System, and transmits an "emergency all-points bulletin" teletype to all concerned law enforcement agencies. The same message text is transmitted by voice via several patch frequencies to all concerned coastal law enforcement agencies.

It is vital that immediately upon receipt of a warning of a tidal wave that the concerned law enforcement agencies initiate evacuation procedures. All persons along the coastal area concerned should be removed at least a mile inland, or to a point of land at least 150 to 250 feet above sea level. Police operations after the tidal wave has struck are similar to those during a flood or hurricane. It becomes even more important to keep crowds of people away from the sea shore after the disaster has struck, as it has frequently occurred that subsequent tidal waves kill many spectators who have flocked to the scene. The police may experience more problems with missing persons during body recovery and identification techniques as tidal waves tend to carry victims many miles out to sea; they are often not recovered.

TRAIN WRECKS

Cause

Most train wrecks involve derailment of the engine or cars of the train. The derailment may be due to a collision at a crossing with other vehicles or a collision between trains. The long stopping distance of trains due to their tremendous weight and momentum often results in their being overdriven as far as the visibility of the engineer is concerned.

Damage Effect

Casualty damage is usually confined to the train which was derailed or the object it struck. The train usually continues in a path parallel to the track, and may be derailed or partly on its side. Deaths and injuries are due to crushing. There are usually far more injuries than deaths.

Related Hazards

With train wrecks, there is always the possibility that another train will come along the same or parallel track and worsen the situation. Additionally, with freight trains there is the ever pres-

Train wrecks have potential for great loss of life, or in the case of freight trains, the possibility of creating a secondary chemical or pollution disaster when dangerous materials are involved. (Photo credit—Bee Newspaper, Modesto, California.)

ent possibility that they are transporting toxic or inflammable chemicals which may be leaking or which may have spilled.

Predicted Frequency

Train wrecks causing injury or death are declining as rail traffic is reduced. Minor train wrecks occur monthly in the United States, usually involving freight trains; but major train wrecks, killing twenty-five or more persons, are now rare.

Police Problems

One of the most important techniques of the police at the scene of the train wreck is the immediate notification of the railroad so that additional trains may be halted. Officers should proceed to a point at least a mile in each direction along the track from the train wreck and be prepared to flag down any approaching train. The universal railroad stop signal is a lighted flare or lantern, swung slowly back and forth horizontally across the tracks. If the engineer sees the signal, he will acknowledge with the traditional two whistle blasts and will attempt to stop the train. If an officer cannot remain in this position, a line of flares across the tracks may be effective.

At the scene of the wreck a check must be made at once for possible spills of chemicals or inflammable materials. The search must be conducted to locate the injured and dead, keeping in mind that injured may be scattered along the road bed for some distance. Most train wrecks occur in isolated areas, and crowd control is a problem only in later stages of the disaster. As a derailed train usually bisects the disaster zone, it may be necessary to establish an ambulance dispatch post on each side of the train wreck.

7
DISASTER CASE STUDIES

In an attempt to further illustrate the nature and course of disasters focusing some of the problems involved in the police response, this chapter will present a selection of case studies. While these case studies differ in format and content, each attempts to portray problems confronted by the police. The case studies were obtained by a combination of interviews, examination of public records, periodicals, newspaper accounts, and correspondence.

THE CRESCENT CITY TIDAL WAVE

The Alaskan earthquake of March 27, 1964 created extensive tidal wave activity along the Pacific Coast. Except for the Alaskan port cities, Crescent City, California suffered the most severe damage. Crescent City is a small lumber community located on Highway U. S. 101, lying just south of the Oregon border. It has a population of approximately 3,000. A series of four tidal waves struck this community, the first occurring just after midnight on March 28, the second at approximately 1:00 AM, the third at 1:40 AM, and the fourth at 2:30 AM.

Twelve persons were killed by drowning, one by heart attack, and several were missing, and are now presumed dead. Twenty-nine blocks of the business district were completely destroyed, at a loss estimated over 27 million dollars. Extensive damage was done to the fishing fleet in the harbor, and the disaster was complicated by an explosion and fire at the Texaco plant. This fire burned for three days. Traffic on U. S. 101 was diverted for five days.

Ample warning of the impending disaster was provided by county sheriffs deputies and city police, through normal communication channels as well as a tidal wave warning alert from the Honolulu, Hawaii observatory. Officers and other civil defense workers were able to conduct evacuation operations in advance of the first tidal wave, which was of a minor nature. The deaths were caused by a later and far more devastating wave, following a pattern set by a number of past tidal waves including Hawaii and Chile in 1960. Evacuated survivors, after several apparently harmless tidal waves, moved back into the low lying area. A later far more powerful wave engulfed them.

Except for evacuation operations and attempts to prevent residents from reentering the area during the period of tidal wave activity, the police operation was largely concerned with the prevention of looting, traffic control, and convergence control. Sheriffs deputies initiated a rowboat security patrol of the areas still under water in an attempt to prevent looting. This operation was taken over by thirty-seven members of the California National Guard by 9:00 AM the morning of the 28th. Police and sheriffs deputies established a cordon of the damaged area, and restricted entry by time pass to daylight hours only. The California Highway Patrol dispatched thirty patrol units from central and southern California to assist in the re-routing of traffic over an alternate route from Highway 101. Only five minor looting cases were experienced. Law enforcement officers were most hampered in their disaster response by a shortage of portable communications equipment, as many of the operations could not be carried out in patrol cars. The communications problem was further complicated when various roads and bridges were destroyed in the final tidal surge, and law enforcement officers were isolated from each other physically.

THE BEL-AIR AND TOPANGA FIRE

On November 6, 1961 two brush fires of major proportions broke out within five hours. Of the two, the Bel-Air fire was the more serious. It originated at a point north of Mulholland Drive near Roscomare Road at 8:10 AM and within half an hour was burning out of control. During the thirty-five hours it remained uncontrolled, it burned through the heavily populated residential communities north of Sunset Boulevard.

The fire crossed, and ran adjacent to, several major surface streets. The terrain in the fire area was mountainous, etched with numerous deep and precipitous ravines, and thickly blanketed with growth of highly flammable brush. High winds and low humidity contributed to the hazardous situation. Few access roads were available to responding services and even fewer lateral or interconnecting streets lay within the emergency area.

A disaster emergency was declared at 10:50 AM. At approximately 1:00 PM the Topanga Canyon fire started just south of Mulholland Drive near the Santa Maria fire road, only six miles west of the point of origin of the Bel-Air fire. This second conflagration, although eventually burning a larger total area, was confined to a sparsely settled region of city and county watershed. It did, however, threaten the populated Pacific Palisades area and necessitated diversion of police manpower from the Bel-Air fire.

Only a small number of minor injuries were reported but 484 dwellings were destroyed or severely damaged, and in Topanga 61 structures were destroyed or severely damaged.

The police role was one of active assistance and service to the affected area. After the initial alarm, the area was quickly surveyed and information of the potential disaster was directed to the Business Office Division, who later activated departmental emergency operations.

Evacuation of the endangered residents was accomplished by officers on a door-to-door basis. Simultaneously, other officers were deployed to establish perimeter control to facilitate and expedite the operations of the fire department attempting to contain and extinguish the fire.

This early action prevented any loss of life and saved many homes from destruction, thus achieving the primary police function. During this period of stress the remainder of the city continued to receive adequate police protection although large numbers of personnel and equipment were diverted to the emergency area.

After the initial needs for service had been met and the fire had left ravaged remains of the once valuable possessions, looters and souvenir hunters began to invade the area, posing a threat to the internal security. Units were immediately deployed to protect the stricken area from thefts.

The steps to be taken in response to such an emergency had been outlined in detail in the *Police Tactical Manual.* Problems of command, communications, deployment, evacuation, restriction of area, and logistics had been anticipated. Guides to their solution were included in the Manual.

The emergency control center was activated at the Los Angeles Police Building at 8:57 AM under the command of the captain of the business office division, and was staffed by officers from the business office, planning and research, and traffic services divisions.

The primary functions of the ECC were to direct and coordinate the department's emergency control activities; to collect and disseminate information from the field command posts, hospitals, and other concerned agencies; to determine the needs of, and provide emergency personnel, equipment, and supplies to, the field commander and the field forces; to maintain chronological logs, situation maps, and situation reports; to request assistance from other agencies when needed by the field commander; and to complete the necessary reports regarding the emergency incident and prepare a final report for submission to the chief of police.

At 8:55 AM, upon request of the Patrol Bureau, the mobile command post was dispatched to the scene of the fire. During most of the emergency, the field commander remained with the mobile command post.

At the outbreak of the emergency there were a total of 316 uniformed personnel on street patrol. Of these, 230 were redeployed to the disaster area. The major police purposes were to maintain effective perimeter control, internal security, evacuation of residents, control of crowds and sightseers, restriction of the emergency area to authorized agencies and personnel, and the establishment and maintenance of ingress and egress routes for these services.

A twelve-hour tour of duty was initiated, days off were cancelled and officers who were on days off were notified to return to duty.

Patrol division commanders were requested to reevaluate their deployment requirements and provide as many men for the emergency as they could without crippling their ability to cope with their routine police requirements.

As the area of the emergency expanded rapidly it was necessary to establish special supervisory positions for line control in addition to the ECC and command post commanders. The following special supervisory positions were established in accordance with the *Unusual Occurrence Manual:* Perimeter Control (traffic and restriction of area); Internal Security Patrol (anti-looting); Evacuation; Press Relations; Personnel Pool; Equipment; Intelligence (scouts); and liaison with other agencies.

THE PACOIMA AIRPLANE CRASH

On January 31, 1957 at 11:20 AM, a Douglas DC-7B was 30,000 feet over the San Fernando Valley on its last test flight before being delivered. At the same altitude a jet interceptor, on a radar checkout mission, was on its last test flight before being turned over to the United States Air Force. The interceptor and the DC-7B collided in mid-air at nearly head-on courses. The interceptor took off eight feet of the left wing of the DC-7B.

The interceptor immediately burst into flames and crashed to the earth in the unpopulated hills. One survivor, the radar operator, managed to eject and bailed out successfully, even though his parachute was afire as he descended. The pilot was killed.

The DC-7B appeared at first stable but when it started descending the pressure and buffeting were too much for the broken wing and the plane began disintegrating. Evidence and witnesses show that the pilot was trying to crash the plane in an open spot. In this case the open spot was a school yard. The bulk of the plane fell on the school yard, the remainder fell on a church yard next door.

Just moments before the crash, 220 boys were routinely called from gym classes on the field. Some of them were still running from the field to the gym when the plane hit. There were 800 students in the auditorium.

Major debris from the plane was scattered over a two block area. The injuries and two of the deaths were the result of flying debris from the plane as it crashed. No fire occurred. There were seven killed and seventy-four injured as a result of the accident; one killed in the interceptor, four crewmen of the DC-7B, and two boys killed in the school yard. Nearly all of the seventy-four injuries were boys who were on the school yard at the time of the crash.

The police, upon becoming aware of the crash, immediately dispatched units to the location and cordoned off a two-block square around the scene. All motorcycle officers in the city were dispatched to the scene to maintain the cordon. Only emergency vehicles were allowed inside the cordon. This cordon was held until the aviation authorities completed their investigation.

One of the first things that the police department did upon learning of the crash was to call the Valley Hospital to prepare for a major disaster. Immediately after this notification, the hospital put its plan for emergencies into operation by calling doctors and nurses. Within minutes they had rounded up forty physicians and all staff nurses.

Ambulances from all sections of the Valley responded. Injured were taken to Sun Valley Emergency Hospital, Encino Hospital, and San Fernando Hospital. A large number of helicopters were called and remained on standby for emergency use.

No particular plan was in effect at the time of the crash. The Los Angeles Police Department did not have, at that time, their *Tactical Manual*, consequently, there was no department recorder on the scene.

THE TWIN NEW YORK AIRPLANE CRASH

A United Air Lines DC-8 jet from Chicago plunged into the crowded Park Slope section of Brooklyn shortly after 10:30 AM, December 17, 1960. All but one of its seventy-seven passengers and the crew of seven were killed at once. The survivor was an 11-year-old boy. He was thrown clear of the wreckage into the snow but he died a day later.

The plane demolished a church and killed a department of sanitation worker who was shoveling snow. Burning debris caused a seven-alarm fire destroying ten brownstone apartment buildings, several shops, and a funeral home. Nine persons were injured on the ground. At almost the same instant as the Brooklyn disaster, a Trans World Airlines Lockheed Super-Constellation crashed near Miller Army Air Field. This plane, out of Columbus, Ohio, exploded in the air just before the crash. All thirty-nine passengers and the crew of five were killed or fatally injured. Three survived the crash but died before they could reach the hospital. Parts of the plane fell in the Lower Bay and parts on the northwest corner of Miller Field.

The two crashes were caused by a mid-air collision. Approaching the city, the United jet was ordered by traffic controllers to fly a holding, or stacking pattern, 5,000 feet over Preston, New Jersey, until cleared to proceed to Idlewild. The T.W.A. plane was directed to fly a holding pattern 6,000 feet over Linden, New Jersey, until cleared for La Guardia. Their courses from the holding pattern to the airports would have been several miles apart. The United Air Lines plane flew about twelve miles beyond its assigned circling area and collided with the Trans World Airlines plane.

Police Commissioner Kennedy broadcast an appeal asking the curious to stay away from the scene, but thousands were drawn to it and police lines had to be formed on all sides. Hundreds of motorists, sightseers and homeward bound commuters added to an already chaotic situation. For miles around the scene, side streets were clogged with autos. Major traffic arteries were closed or partly closed to clear paths for the emergency vehicles responding to the scenes. The same poor weather that was apparently a factor in the accident aided police, fire, and hospital vehicles, for it kept away many motorists who would normally be on the roads.

As dusk approached, the fire department put its emergency searchlight units into action while hundreds of firemen and policemen continued to search the rubble and wreckage turning up bits of evidence to help identify the victims. They were still finding bodies in the wreckage two days after the crash.

As for traffic, by 7:00 PM the traffic situation was back to normal. The major traffic arteries which were closed or partly closed were reopened by 4:00 PM to homeward bound motorists.

For fifteen minutes after the disaster police and firemen did not know they were dealing with the wreckage of a giant jet airliner. They thought at first that a propeller plane had crashed and that no more than a dozen persons were aboard. Not until the arrival of aviation accident investigators was it indicated that scores of persons lay dead in the wreckage.

A few minutes after the first alarm was flashed into police headquarters, thirty-nine patrol cars, four emergency rescue trucks and 265 policemen were at the Brooklyn crash. On Staten Island, the police forces included eighteen patrol cars, three emergency trucks and 136 men. There were also three police helicopters from Floyd Bennett Field hovering over the scene. Communications were taken care of by two police radio trucks and a telephone switchboard trailer, lent by the New Jersey Bell Telephone Company. Because debris littered the Lower Bay off New York, it was feared some plane victims might be in the water. Four police launches, with fifteen men aboard, joined the futile search. After the extent of the disaster was apparent, 250 auxiliary policemen were ordered out. Seven hundred policemen had been mobilized within ninety minutes in the Park Slope section.

The police department received an enormous amount of assistance. Five fire alarms were rung in Brooklyn firehouses and two in Manhattan for the Brooklyn crash. Fifty-six pieces of apparatus—pumpers, ladder trucks, rescue trucks, searchlight trucks and a radio truck—went to the Sterling blaze set off by the crash.

Nearly three hundred off-duty firemen had voluntarily come to the scene to help their comrades, about equal in number who were already there. A city-wide disaster signal was turned in. This brought five hundred men and women civilians, trained as auxiliary policemen, firemen, first-aid men, drivers, messengers, and nurses to the scene. Two mobile communications trucks were set up at the Brooklyn site by civilian defense workers.

Kings County Hospital sent four ambulances, twenty doctors, eight nurses, and eight attendants to the Brooklyn scene. Bellevue Hospital's similar disaster unit went first to Staten Island and then to Brooklyn. A score of city and voluntary hospitals in Brooklyn also sent ambulances, doctors, and nurses to Sterling Place, but there was little for them to do.

Red Cross and Salvation Army units were giving hot coffee, soup, and doughnuts to disaster workers. Welfare department workers were on hand to assist those evacuated from the stricken buildings. Many of the homeless were congregated in the lobbies of nearby theaters and churches.

The first rescuers at the Staten Island crash were artillery men and aircraft maintenance men stationed at Miller Field. Since the crash was on an open, little-used airfield and the fire less serious than in Brooklyn, there was a much smaller mobilization of disaster teams on Staten Island.

Seaview Hospital sent its disaster team of three ambulances. Fifty doctors responded, but only the three fatally injured persons were in need of medical aid and they were taken to the hospital. Twenty-five Coast Guard boats with a total of two hundred men aboard then searched the Lower Bay for victims.

Many helpful passers-by did their best to rescue victims at the Brooklyn scene. Physicians from "doctors row," Brooklyn's Eighth Avenue, rushed to the scene but found little to do.

The police completely blocked off the area with wooden barricades to keep the people away and also so that the evidence could be gathered concerning the causes of the crash. They also evacuated all tenants whose lives may have been in danger either from fire or the damage of the crash.

The New York police department Mobilization Plan works to speed required police strength to the scene, and uses a series of code signals, each of which causes a predetermined number of men, mobile and specialized equipment to respond at once. Its dual purposes are to redeploy manpower in sufficient strength to meet a critical police need and to effect the build-up in a rapid yet orderly manner and without stripping bordering precincts and outlying areas of essential police service. The code-signal system, which catalyzes the plan, contains certain safeguards against indiscriminate redeployment of manpower on patrol. The basic code signal 10-41, which requests three sergeants and fifteen patrolmen, may be activated by a first-line superior. If signals of a higher order are to be used, they must be transmitted in sequence, resulting in a cumulative response of personnel. Generally, the greater the magnitude of men and equipment to respond, the higher the authority required.

THE MADISON RIVER CANYON EARTHQUAKE (YELLOWSTONE)

In the Hebgen Lake area, the night of August 17, 1959, the resorts and campgrounds were filled with vacationers, many of whom were camped downstream from Hebgen Dam in the narrow confines of the Madison River Canyon.

At about 11:37 that night, at least three blocks of the earth's crust suddenly subsided, and a major earthquake was felt in the area. The ground lurched and trembled; man-made structures were fractured, and in places shattered and collapsed. People, shaken awake, rushed outside wondering what had happened. Many persons, stunned by the shock, gaped unbelievingly at the newly formed features. Hebgen Lake, jostled by the abrupt drop, began to slosh back and forth in great waves, the first few of which were large enough to flow over Hebgen Dam.

In the Madison River Canyon near the Rock Creek campground, part of a mountainside was shattered by the major tremor, and for a few brief seconds hung poised over the unsuspecting, awakened campers. A few lay sleepily in their tents or trailers wondering what had happened; most assumed that the shaking of their tents and trailers was caused by bears. Several persons went out to investigate, but in the clear moonlight everything seemed normal. Suddenly, with a terrible roaring and grinding noise, the entire mountainside began to move. As the campers tried to flee, the avalanche slid into the canyon moving at nearly one hundred miles an hour. People, cars, and trailers were crushed and buried. The survivors were knocked down by a violent air blast, and then some of them were engulfed by a huge wave of water from the displaced Madison River.

Working in the pitch-black darkness to rescue the trapped and injured, survivors of the catastrophe constantly felt the earth trembling beneath their feet as repeated aftershocks shook the area. Boulders and rockfalls could be heard tumbling down the mountainsides.

When day dawned, the immensity of the landslide became apparent to the chilled and shaken watchers huddled on the slopes, but it was a long time afterward before the toll of human life was established. No one knew how many people had been camped in and near the Rock Creek campground prior to the disaster.

Following the main shock of the earthquake, escape routes were blocked. A huge landslide sealed the lower end of the canyon. Slip-outs in the highway skirting Hebgen Lake effectively stopped escape in that direction.

Communication lines were out. First reports of the disaster came from a "ham" radio operator in badly damaged West Yellowstone. He had little knowledge of what had happened in the Madison Canyon. All that was known for sure was that there was chaos; there was a threat of flood; and there were trapped people desperately in need of help.

Help was on the way before dawn. Rescue units from many agencies in Idaho and Montana were on the move. At dawn a plane made a reconnaissance flight. Forest Service smokejumpers parachuted into the canyon to give first aid and to set up communications. Men on foot, on horseback, and in helicopters moved in to give assistance to survivors. Among the refugees themselves there were many outstanding acts of brotherhood and mutual help. Rescue workers treated the injured and evacuated them to nearby towns and ranches, where other volunteers provided food and shelter. By evening bulldozer roads had been built around highway slipouts; the immediate emergency was over, and all who wished to leave were able to get out of the canyon.

Some thirty-four federal, state, county and local agencies and organizations participated in the emergency work following the earthquake. Neighboring states and Canadian Provinces offered further assistance. The search and rescue efforts of all groups, coordinated by Forest Service officers, continued until there could be no doubt that anyone was still stranded or lost. Only twenty-eight lives were lost as a result of the earthquake.

THE INDIANA FAIRGROUNDS EXPLOSION

A blast ripped out a fifty foot section of box seats at the east end of the arena. Giant chunks of concrete from the basic structure of the arena were hurled into the air and came down on the spectators. The seats in the immediate area of the blast held 368 persons. Of that number, 128 were in box seats above the explosion. Some 240 were in temporary seats beneath the tumbling concrete block and seats. The blast hurled the entire box section into the air and down again into the bleachers.

The audience was estimated at six thousand persons. The coliseum seats about twice that number. The exterior of the building remained intact.

Reports from the State Fire Marshal's Office indicated that a broken valve on a tank of butane gas had caused a leak of volatile fumes that were touched off by contact with a heating or cooking flame in a nearby concession stand.

The blast occurred at 11:06 PM. Had the show started on time instead of fifteen minutes late, most of the victims would have left the arena. As the uninjured groped for exits, a second blast erupted out of the yawning hole already filled with twisted seats, chunks of concrete and bodies. Both blasts were over within a two minute period. The number of dead in the explosion was 68 and 381 persons were injured.

Bleeding or dazed, some people wandered aimlessly out of the coliseum. Some fled wildly across the ice, slipping and skidding as they tried to escape. Others clawed with their bare hands to drag away five hundred pound blocks of concrete that pinned people in the wreckage. The auditorium, brilliantly illuminated by spotlights, echoed with screams of the injured, some lying helplessly trapped beneath bodies of the dead.

Many of those not seriously injured lined up at telephone booths to let relatives know they had survived. The band continued playing as the screaming crowd sought refuge. Officials credited their coolness with averting worse casualties through a mass panic. The rescue workers worked through the night in uncovering bodies and identifying the dead. By morning, all but two of the dead were identified. The Marion County Coroner called for a large truck to gather personal belongings—mink stoles, billfolds, purses and clothing—scattered across the bloody ice and debris.

The Indianapolis Police Department had 175 men assigned to first-aid and rescue work. A communications headquarters and master control center was set up on the outside, and a portable control unit was brought right onto the ice's edge. A general command post, with commanders of the Indianapolis Police Department, Indiana State Police, and Marion County Sheriff's Office, was set up immediately. The communications branch of the Indianapolis Police Department contacted all local hopitals, and all available medical personnel rushed immediately to their hospitals to take care of the injured.

The police impounded four undamaged tanks of the propane gas for examination by experts, including one from the T. P. Gas Association in Boston.

The Indiana state police and the Marion County Sheriff's Office sent all available personnel. A temporary morgue was set up right on the ice. Rows of bodies were lined up under blankets on the ice and other rows were started outside the building in a drizzling rain.

The injured were being taken to several Indianapolis hospitals in taxis, ambulances, cars, and buses. Methodist Hospital near the scene was quickly jammed with at least forty injured. Stretchers packed the hospital halls. A radio appeal for blood met immediate response as the injured were taken to six hospitals. By dawn it was reported there were more voluntary donors than were needed at some hospitals.

Every available ambulance, even a dog-kennel wagon, was summoned. Auto wreckers arrived to lift huge concrete chunks the size of grand pianos off some of the pinned-down victims. Finally, two big construction cranes were brought in. Hundreds of firemen, civil defense, Red Cross, and Salvation Army workers, and doctors and nurses arrived at the scene to help with the victims.

The main police action was rescue, first aid, and getting the victims to the hospitals. Being that the coliseum is located five miles away from the civic center, they did not have much of a problem with traffic and did not have to cordon off the area because the coliseum is located in a totally isolated area.

THE BAKERSFIELD EARTHQUAKE

One month after the Arvin-Tehachapi earthquake (July 21, 1952) a second disastrous quake struck the city of Bakersfield on August 22, 1952 at 3:48 PM. The amount of damage caused by the first quake was limited, but the second caused considerably more damage. The earthquake centered in a locale about five miles east of Bakersfield. The velocity measured a magnitude of 9.0 on the scale, producing sharp "jolts" for ten seconds.

Major damage occurred in the downtown area of Bakersfield with tons of bricks falling in the streets. Although thousands of persons were on the city streets at the time, only two were killed and thirty-nine injured. Damage centered around larger buildings, such as hotels and multi-story business. Overall damage in the area was estimated between 10 and 30 million dollars. Many farms in the outlying area had major loss because of the amount of damage done to irrigation pipes, wells, pumps, farming equipment, and crops as well.

Disruption of conditions occurred more in the business district of downtown Bakersfield rather than in the community as a whole. The downtown was closed for two weeks following the quake allowing only owners and workers in the area. Many businesses opened after the two-week period, but a large number were condemned by building inspectors.

Reserve officers and off-duty personnel had reported to the scene of the earthquake within thirty minutes of its occurrence. These men had been previously instructed to report directly to the scene of the disaster. Officers from the sheriff's office and the

California Highway Patrol were also available. Police action included sending search teams into the area, setting up barricades, diverting traffic—automobile and pedestrian—and evacuating the area. Rescue operations were turned over to the fire department after the initial search by the police. A police pass system was set up which allowed workers into the area, later store owners and residents.

The police manpower call-up was efficient because of prior instructions to reserve and off-duty officers for emergency situations. There was no problem in command succession due to the number of personnel available and the confined area. There was no delay in obtaining needed equipment and materials for the operation.

THE ARVIN-TEHACHAPI EARTHQUAKE

On July 21, 1952, 4:52 AM an earthquake originated in southern California radiating tremors that extended as far south as the Mexican border, north to San Francisco, and east to Nevada. Tremors were felt for a period of forty-five seconds (the duration of the earthquake). The original starting point of the quake centered between two small mountain towns, Arvin and Tehachapi, located approximately seventy-five miles northwest of Los Angeles. Seismologists have given the exact location at a point four miles southeast of Arvin and fifteen miles northwest of Tehachapi.

A slippage of five to fifteen feet caused a crack in the earth's crust. This crack produced a velocity of 10,000 mph and registered a magnitude of 7.5. The Arvin-Tehachapi earthquake has been considered the worst quake since the San Francisco earthquake of 1906, which registered 8.25.

A total of thirteen persons were killed in Tehachapi and thirty-five injured. In the city of Arvin one person was killed and twenty-five injured. Property damage for Tehachapi was estimated to be 2,500,000 dollars. Most of the damage occurred in the Tehachapi business district, destroying 85 per cent of the district. Included in this area were thirty-one businesses, three public facilities, one church, one hospital, and nineteen residences.

Compared to Tehachapi, the amount of property damage in Arvin was far less extensive. There is no exact figure available for the estimated cost, but several buildings and residential homes were damaged considerably; fourteen business buildings were condemned as a result of the earthquake.

Disruption in community living conditions resulted when all power and sources of communication were temporarily cut off. Inhabitants of the area were compelled to walk for miles to telephone for assistance. All roads leading into Tehachapi were temporarily closed. Necessary equipment, doctors, and nurses had to be flown into the area by the Air Force. Miles of railroad tracks were destroyed, thereby discontinuing regular train service for a period of thirty days. About three weeks later the disaster roads were open and businesses set up adequate facilities for minimum trading.

Police action at the time of the earthquake was very limited due to the fact that there was only one policeman in the town. Temporary action came from civil defense workers who immediately set up barricades and looting patrols. More direct and permanent action was taken over by the army units upon their arrival. They assumed the task of issuing passes to workers and residents of the area. Their major problem was in controlling the number of sightseers approaching the area.

THE SANTA FE TRAIN WRECK

On January 22, 1956 a Santa Fe passenger train (No. 83) left the Los Angeles Union Station at 5:30 PM. At approximately 5:40 PM the train overturned while negotiating a turn. The cause of the accident was due in part to the excessive speed of the train while attempting to make the turn, estimated at a speed of 69 mph, for a curve that had been designated for a maximum speed of 15 mph. The engineer of the train was suffering a temporary blackout at the time of the wreck. Therefore, he was unaware of the increasing speed of the train. The accident occurred in the railroad yards taking in the area west of Soto Street, east of Santa Fe Avenue, and north of Washington Boulevard.

At the time of the accident the train was carrying a total of 167 persons—161 passengers and a crew of six. Of this total 30 were killed and 135 injured. The surrounding area consisted entirely of industries, thereby causing no disruption in community living. However, from the onset of the accident at 5:40 PM to 1:00 AM (January 23, 1956), at which time the wrecked train was righted and removed, there was very heavy congestion within the immediate railroad yard area.

The Los Angeles Police Department was first notified of the wreck at 5:51 PM. The notification was received through the complaint board, who immediately dispatched an ambulance and traffic investigation unit into the area.

Times of importance were as follows:

January 22
    6:00 PM: Additional units dispatched upon request.
    6:03 PM: Sigalert broadcast.
    6:15 PM: Units sent to divert traffic at Soto Street and Washington Blvd., also at Santa Fe and Washington Blvd.
    6:45 PM: All injured persons removed from scene.

January 23
    1:00 AM: Wrecked train righted and removed.
    8:00 AM: Coroner's examination of scene; command post closed.

The number of policemen sent from the Los Angeles Police Department at the scene of the wreck totaled three hundred; 25 per cent assigned to traffic control on the perimeter. An additional forty-five officers were received from the Los Angeles County Sheriffs and also twenty-five from the National Guard who volunteered their assistance.

Action taken by the police included the following: a) aiding in the removal of injured and dead from the scene; b) directing traffic at specified points to alleviate congestion; c) controlling the flow of emergency equipment; and d) controlling the pedestrian traffic which had entered the yard on foot.

The amount of manpower available was sufficient but not very efficient for the task at hand. This was due in part to the fact that there was no plan in existence prior to the train wreck. A previously established plan would have set forth an immediate method of operation. When a command post was finally established, officers arriving did not report there but went directly to the disaster area. This hampered overall effectiveness because officers in command did not know exactly how many men were arriving or who they were. By failing to report to the command post and communicate with the officers in charge, further problems occurred, such as securing additional officers to relieve men already on duty and also providing the men with food and necessary equipment.

There was a slight delay in obtaining necessary equipment due to the location of the wreck and the condition of the road. Ambulances had some difficulty in approaching the area. The wreck occurred on private property and directions were not specific.

There was some problem in command succession at the onset because officers were arriving from three geographical divisions almost immediately. Supervisors also arriving from the three divisions delayed in briefing each other on the situation before establishing the command post. Such a short briefing period would have avoided conflict between commands. However, command succession ceased to be a problem once the command post was established.

THE BALDWIN HILLS RESERVOIR DAM BURST

On December 14, 1963 at 3:35 PM, a portion of a wall of the dam which supports a reservoir in the Baldwin Hills area collapsed, inundating an area of approximately 262 acres north of the reservoir. The area's geographical boundaries include: Ballona Creek on the west, La Brea Avenue on the east, a varying line running from Coliseum Street to Rodeo Road on the south, and a varying line from Bowesfield Street to Sunlight Place on the north. The major or deep water area was bounded by Redondo Boulevard on the east, Hauser Boulevard on the west, Coliseum Street on the south, and Rodeo Road on the north.

At 11:30 AM, December 14, 1963, the caretaker for the stated reservoir noticed an excessive flow of water from the overflow pipes. At 1:10 PM a Water and Power engineer noticed that the damage to the reservoir had increased from internal damage to a discernible external crack in the bottom portion of the northern earth. At 3:35 PM the crack near the northeast corner of the reservoir had widened and the dam in that entire area was collapsing. The break in the wall enlarged to an opening extending from the top of the reservoir to the bottom. The dam ruptured at 3:35 PM and by 5:25 PM initial, intense flooding conditions had sufficiently subsided. By 6:50 PM it was possible to bring in necessary equipment for clean-up operations.

The Baldwin Hills Reservoir disaster left a total of five persons dead and twenty-five injured; six of which were policemen. Damage was done to 547 main structures, many of them multiple unit apartment buildings. Seventeen parcels of both land and buildings were completely washed away. In addition, some twenty other homes were destroyed beyond repair; fifty lots partially washed away; and fifty-five building structures severely damaged. Two large shopping centers, one at La Brea and Rodeo Road and the other at La Cienega and Rodeo Road, also suffered damage because of the disaster. Total assessed value of the real property in the area exceeded 16 million dollars, indicating a market value of somewhere between 64 and 65 million dollars. Unaccounted for are the figures showing an estimate of personal property loss, and the number of vehicles destroyed or washed away. However, insurance coverage in the area indicates approximately 1,600 vehicles were badly damaged.

Community disruption started at 1:45 PM when evacuation of residents in the area began. At 3:10 PM the area between La Cienega and La Brea, and Jefferson and the reservoir was closed off completely. The electric power was cut off at 3:44 PM, remaining off for a total of three hours and twelve minutes. Residents who lived in the area were not allowed to return to their homes until 10:30 PM of the same evening, and then on foot only. The area was closed to through traffic until the early morning hours of December 17. Normal patrol of the area was not resumed until December 23.

The Los Angeles Police Department first received notification at 1:12 PM in the form of a complaint from a citizen who was concerned about an excessive flow of water and the possibility of a broken water main.

Times of importance were as follows:
1:30 PM: Water and Power supervisor advised that the reservoir was about to break.

1:35 PM: Patrol unit responded to citizen's complaint; advised to check the base of the dam. Sergeant's unit also dispatched.
1:45 PM: Broadcast went out to all available units to start evacuation of area.
1:55 PM: Mobile command post en route to scene accompanied by twenty-five motor officers.
2:28 PM: Sigalert notification for evacuation.
2:55 PM: Dorsey High School manned by Red Cross as an evacuation center.
3:10 PM: Area closed under section 409.5 P.C.
3:30 PM: Evacuation of area completed with exception of few persons refusing to leave.
3:35 PM: Dam burst.
3:40 PM: All day-watch personnel held over.
5:00 PM: All traffic diverted from La Brea and Jefferson, Stocker and La Brea, Stocker and La Cienega, Wrightcrest and La Cienega, and Jefferson and La Cienega.
5:25 PM: Command post established at Jefferson and La Brea.
6:30 PM: Policing of area underway. Scouting and looting units sent into area.
7:06 PM: Water and power services resumed.
10:30 PM: Sufficient control maintained to allow pedestrian passes for residents.
10:40 PM: Eighty man perimeter established and patrol details established.

Outside assistance was received from the California Highway Patrol, Los Angeles County Sheriffs, and Culver City Police Department, primarily to aid in diverting traffic. Helicopters from the Los Angeles Fire Department, Coast Guard, and United States Marine Corps, along with Life Guards from Los Angeles County and Santa Monica, were also called in to assist in rescue operations.

The supply of manpower made available was both sufficient and efficient. Field officers and officers from staff and command rank were made available from divisional assignments and were utilized effectively. The one shortcoming in manpower was in second-level supervision. Looting and scouting patrols were commanded by sergeants who had a range of fifteen to twenty men under their supervision. The span of control was frequently too wide. At the onset of the disaster there was no problem in command succession. This was due in part to a plan already in existence prior to the disaster which established procedures to follow in such an event.

One problem in communication was the lack of an adequate number of walkie-talkies. Many areas could be approached on foot only due to the mud and debris, and information regarding these areas was slow in arriving at the command post. The total loss for the police department included three police vehicles and twenty-six police motorcycles.

THE SOUTH AMBOY PORT EXPLOSION

On Friday, May 19, 1950 at about 7:26 PM an explosion of tremendous violence occurred at the "powder pier" (Pier 4) at the foot of Augusta Street, South Amboy, New Jersey. This explosion was caused by the simultaneous detonation of 150 tons of military explosives and gelatin dynamite. Twenty-six Healing Company employees and five coal barge captains were killed (remains of only a few bodies were recovered), and more than 350 residents of South Amboy and Perth Amboy were injured by the blast. The four lighters, the "powder pier" and the railroad cars, and piers and equipment in the adjoining waterfront area were demolished. Many of the seventeen barges in the port area were set on fire or sunk. Mangled coal gondola cars and twisted girders of the heavy, coal-loader structures gave graphic evidence of the violence of the explosion. Complete failure of electric power darkened the town, windows were blown out amid a rain of debris, and terror and confusion reigned throughout the small community. Property damage extended over a distance of twenty-five miles from the scene of the explosion.

The explosion blast rushed upon the communities of South Amboy and Perth Amboy with a tremendous surge. The damage was extensive—windows were smashed in almost every one of 2700 buildings and homes of South Amboy. The nearby city of Perth Amboy and its 2200 homes sustained similar damage. People fled their homes into rain-drenched streets, some of them suffering from the concussion and some cut by flying sections of glass. Many of the persons could remember the two previous explosions which had struck South Amboy. The thought of an atomic bomb was undoubtedly in the minds of some people. A mushroom-shaped cloud of smoke from explosion could be seen hanging over the port area. The explosion was felt by many persons in points as far as Trenton, thirty-five miles away. A single shock wave was recorded on the seismograph at Fordham University, more than thirty miles away in the upper Bronx, at 7:25:56 PM.

Emergency operations went into effect directly after the explosion. Police and fire units were called into action. The Coast Guard alerted all available personnel and sent harbor craft to the scene. The New York City Harbor Police also sent boats. The fires in the coal barges were fought by Coast Guard and New York City fire boats. Mayor John D. Leonard declared a state of emergency at 7:50 PM and sent out a call for help. The effects of the explosion were felt over such a wide area that it was immediately apparent to nearby communities that a major catastrophe had occurred and that assistance would be needed. South Amboy had no organized Civil Defense Plan in effect and was immediately confronted with the problem of seeking aid from the state. The New Jersey State Police responded immediately after receipt of a radio call from a state police officer who resided in South Amboy, and Governor Alfred E. Driscoll ordered that the facilities of the state be made available. Thirty-five fire companies from all over New Jersey responded and first aid squads from about fifty localities as far off as Marcus Hook, Pennsylvania, were brought in by teletyped police messages and radio announcements. These emergency calls also brought response from the Army at Fort Monmouth, the National Guard, and a detachment of Marines from the Naval Ammunition Depot at Earle to patrol the town, restore order, and prevent looting. Communications were temporarily disrupted over a five-mile area and radio amateurs aided by relaying urgent messages. The New Jersey Bell Telephone Company sent five mobile telephone trucks from Newark to handle the increased calls to police and hospitals. Scores of doctors and hundreds of nurses responded to the emergency calls.

A period of panic lasted about twenty minutes. Orderly actions were thereafter impressed upon the public. The nearby schools were thrown open for shelter. Sound trucks cruised the glass-littered streets, informing the residents of the nature of the explosion, warning them not to touch any suspicious-looking objects that might be live mines, and directing them to go home calmly and shut off gas jets and pilot lights as a precaution. No fires were reported other than the burning coal barges on the waterfront.

First aid field units were established in the streets of South Amboy and Perth Amboy to provide emergency treatment. The severely injured were removed to hospitals in South Amboy, Perth Amboy, New Brunswick, and Parlin. The American Red Cross and Salvation Army quickly mobilized disaster relief facilities, providing food and shelter to many of the victims. Fire companies were ordered to stand by at local fire houses. The first aid squads were directed to a central point at the railroad plaza. Police and first aid operations were directed from the South Amboy City Hall. Local municipal agencies went to work checking on public services. Lights were quickly restored; water and gas mains were not affected by the blast. By 1:00 AM the situation was declared under control.

Meanwhile investigators and technical experts were entering the devastated port area. It was soon obvious that very few bodies would be recovered, as Pier 4 and all of the lighters were completely demolished. The specter of further loss of life loomed when it was discovered that thousands of unexploded antipersonnel mines were scattered throughout the area. Safety to all personnel was a primary objective and the danger area was immediately placed under guard and closed until daybreak. Expert United States Army Engineers' disposal crews from Governors Island and Camp Devens, Massachusetts, and officers from the United States Naval Ammunition Depot at Earle were called in, and a concentrated effort of "mine sweeping," to rid the area of unexploded mines, was commenced. Mine detectors were utilized to find the mines which were buried in the debris and neighboring coal piles. Army medical orderlies stood by in the event that one of the mines might explode and injure a squad member. Nearby power plant operators expressed grave concern for 15,000 tons of stored coal in the yard area and made plans to screen the fuel before transfer to boilers. By good fortune, this coal pile provided an effective barricade, minimizing the damage to the power plant. As the explosives were collected, they were detonated in a guarded area away from the inhabited sections of the city.

One of the anti-personnel mines was found in the coal tender of a railroad locomotive three weeks later, on Friday, June 9. The fortunate discovery prevented a possible train wreck. The train was stopped and passengers were asked to leave until the coal could be thoroughly searched for additional mines.

On Sunday afternoon, May 21, a fire started at the phosphorus plant of the American Agricultural Chemical Company, as a result of exposure to the air of phosphorus in explosion-damaged drums. This plant was approximately 1200 feet from the explosion scene. The river side of the plant was customarily used as a storage area, and, on the day of the blast, 105 drums, each containing 363 pounds of phosphorus, were stored. Approximately forty of these large drums became involved in the fire which lasted about twenty hours. More than fifty of the anti-personnel mines which had fallen in the vicinity exploded intermittently during the course of the fire, throwing the burning phosphorus and deadly shrapnel throughout the area. The scattered mines and the copious white clouds of toxic fumes prevented firemen from advancing close to the burning drums. The acrid, irritating smoke was at first carried out over the bay, but during the night the wind increased and changed direction, causing billows of smoke to roll over the nearby highways and temporarily suspending traffic. The blaze was fought from a safe distance for twenty hours before it was brought under control. Fortunately the plant was isolated and the fire could not spread or cause damage to the surrounding properties. On Monday morning, the South Amboy firemen, guided by the regular plant personnel, were able to advance into the dangerous area and apply hose streams to the blazing drums and extinguish them. However, it was necessary to play the water intermittently onto these projectile-riddled drums for many hours in order to prevent spontaneous re-ignition.

It is reported that fire resulted when the perforated drums released their water seals. The phosphorus, drying out on exposure to the heat of the sun, reacted radily with atmospheric oxygen to evolve heat and then fire.

The mine sweeping operations continued for several days. Most of the industrial activity in the port area was brought to a halt until this was completed. The heaviest concentration of about 5800 anti-personnel mines out of the original shipment of 20,000, was located within four days in the port area within a half-mile of the explosion. The mines were found in great numbers in the vicinity of the chemical works and the power plant. Only fifty were found in the business and residential sections of the city. Most of these mines were damaged and some were reported to be in such condition as to be extremely sensitive. Only a few pieces of the 40,000 anti-tank mines were recovered.

An eight-cylinder diesel engine, believed to have been blown from the lighter "Eugene Healing," was found in two pieces on the grounds of the chemical works at four hundred and six hundred yard distances from the pier.

After the initial shock and fright subsided, rehabilitation was begun the next day in earnest. One of the biggest tasks facing the townspeople was the replacement of tons of window glass which had been shattered by the explosion. By Saturday night many of the damaged windows were temporarily covered with transparent plastic sheeting, tar-paper, or were boarded up with wallboard and conditions in the town were gradually quieted. A reduction of troops and police on duty followed. Within the next day or two, hundreds of workmen and truckloads of glass were sent into the cities of South Amboy and Perth Amboy in order to facilitate this work.

South Amboy is located near an area experiencing heavy traffic on weekends, and preparations were made with military and state police to control the Sunday traffic towards the town. To prevent infiltration of curious onlookers, a pass system was established and traffic diverted in an orderly manner. This action was announced over the radio to curb further traffic congestion. Careful inspections were made of the food, water, sewerage, and other essential public facilities in the Amboys by the State of New Jersey Departments of Health and Labor.

With conditions greatly improved on Sunday, the troops were removed and the military and state police were reduced to thirty. Because of increased activities on Monday, this special police staff was raised to eighty. Large-scale operations were also started to clear up the waterfront. The emergency was declared ended on Tuesday. The military demolition squads continued their operations for three more days, until Friday, May 26.

APPENDICES

A
CALIFORNIA MUTUAL AID PLAN

A description of a system for statewide mutual aid, developed in 1967 by the California Disaster Office, is presented as a model for state coordination of mutual aid activities and planning.

I. INTRODUCTION

This Plan is designed to facilitate the mobilization, organization, and operations of the law enforcement resources within the state so as to most effectively minimize the effects of natural or war-caused disasters. It supersedes Annex 11, Law Enforcement Services, of the California Civil Defense and Disaster Plan dated January, 1958, and Annex 11-OP of the California Civil Defense Operations Plan dated March, 1959, and the Law Enforcement Mutual Aid Plan dated June 15, 1961, and is issued under the authority of Section 1507, Military and Veterans Code and the Civil Defense Act of 1950.

The first resource available to you in time of local peril, disaster, or extreme emergency arising out of riot, fire, storm, air pollution, earthquake, or enemy attack, is existing local law enforcement agencies (see Attachment No. 1, Ch. 1, Div. 7, Art. 1, Sec. 1505 Military and Veterans Code). To obtain the assistance of outside agencies, under the provisions of law and the Law Enforcement Mutual Aid Plans:

> Chief of police, to obtain law enforcement assistance from other jurisdictions, shall request assistance through the sheriff of his county.
>
> Chief of police or sheriff, if required to obtain additional law enforcement assistance from outside of the county, shall request assistance through his Regional Law Enforcement Coordinator (see Attachment No. 2).
>
> Regional Law Enforcement Coordinators shall first utilize the law enforcement resources within the region and then, if necessary, request additional law enforcement assistance from other regions

through the Law Enforcement Division of the California Disaster Office.

The local officials requesting assistance to combat a situation of local peril, disaster or extreme emergency, shall remain in full command of the situation and of all nonmilitary resources and personnel responding to the request for assistance. If regular, reserve, and mutual aid law enforcement resources are unable to cope with the situation of local peril, disaster or extreme emergency, the Director of the California Disaster Office will, upon notification from the Regional Law Enforcement Coordinator, the sheriff of a county, or the chief official of a city, request the governor to direct the Adjutant General of California to commit available resources of the California National Guard in support of local law enforcement officials.

Military resources committed to the support of local governmental agencies will remain under military command and control at all times; however, the military commander will accept missions from responsible civil officials.

II. PURPOSES

The purposes of this Plan are the following:

A. To provide for the coordination of the dispatch and use of law enforcement personnel and equipment whenever, because of riot, civil disturbance, enemy action, disaster, or any other cause, a local law enforcement agency requires the dispatch to it of law enforcement assistance from any other jurisdiction.

B. To provide for the coordination of law enforcement planning, operations, and mutual aid on a statewide, regional, operational area, county, and city basis, and to relate such plans to the overall State plan for disaster and emergency operations.

C. To provide for a system for the receipt and dissemination of information, data, and directives pertaining to the law enforcement activities between local agencies.

D. To prescribe a procedure for the inventory of all law enforcement personnel, facilities, and equipment in the State of California.

E. Collect and disseminate information and intelligence relating to riots and civil disturbances, either existing or pending, to the executive officer of the State Government, and to other state agencies which may be called upon to support law enforcement efforts and utilize the information and intelligence to pre-plan distribution and allocation of state resources in support of the overall law enforcement mission.

III. ASSUMPTIONS

Law enforcement functions under disaster conditions are basically the same as those performed in normal operations, except that problems are multiplied. A disaster situation would require resources in manpower and equipment in addition to those normally available and the establishment of priorities in the employment of all available resources.

IV. DEFINITIONS

When used in this plan various words and phrases shall be defined as follows:

Day-to-Day Mutual Aid. Aid performed in accordance with local mutual aid agreements on a voluntary basis or in time of local peril.

Emergency Mutual Aid. Mutual aid rendered after a State of Disaster or a State of Extreme Emergency has been declared by the Governor.

State Law Enforcement Coordinator. That person appointed by the Governor to serve in such capacity.

Regional Law Enforcement Coordinator. That person selected to act in such capacity in any region of the State by the operational area law enforcement coordinators of a region.

Operational Area Law Enforcement Coordinator. The person selected to act in such capacity in any operational area in accordance with procedures established in such area.

Mutual Aid Region. An area of the State designated by the Governor in accordance with the authority contained in the California Disaster Act.

Operational Area. A city and county, or a county and the municipal jurisdictions therein.

V. BASIC POLICIES

A. Law enforcement officers are responsible for the protection of life and property and for the preservation of public peace and order.

B. The law enforcement service, in the disaster and civil defense program, includes all sheriffs' offices, police departments, state agencies having law enforcement responsibilities and facilities, and all regularly constituted peace officers.

C. The primary responsibility of the California Highway Patrol is traffic control and supervision. The California Highway Patrol may provide law enforcement and traffic control assistance in accordance with any plan developed in conjunction with a sheriff or chief of police, or an operational area, regional, or state law enforcement coordinator. Resources committed to the support of local government will, whenever possible, remain under the control and command of the California Highway Patrol; however, commanders and designated supervisors may accept missions from the responsible local officials.
D. Maximum utilization of existing law enforcement resources, prior to the initiation of mutual aid requests, is the basis of effective operations.
E. Existing law enforcement personnel should be supplemented by an adequate number of trained auxiliary or reserve personnel for civil defense or disaster duty.
F. During a state of extreme emergency, state of disaster or local peril, each city, city and county, county operational area, and state law enforcement agency shall render law enforcement mutual aid as herein provided. However, no city, city and county, county, or state law enforcement agency shall be required to deplete unreasonably its own law enforcement resources in furnishing mutual aid hereunder.
G. In the event that the Governor proclaims a state of extreme emergency, he shall have complete authority over all law enforcement activities within the affected area.
H. Emergency law enforcement procedures should be substantially the same as those followed in day-to-day operations.
I. Existing law enforcement telephone, teletype, and radio communications facilities will be used to the fullest possible extent. Requests for mutual aid and other law enforcement communications traffic will be given a high priority for transmission through other secure channels of communication.
J. Each law enforcement agency should provide for alternate and supplemental communications facilities for use during emergency operations.
K. A maximum effort shall be made to provide each successive level of authority with complete, current, and accurate information relating to situations, in progress or anticipated, which may require law enforcement mutual aid or state agency assistance to local law enforcement.

VI. ORGANIZATION

A. Cities and counties
   1. The basis of organization at the city and county level is the police department or sheriff's office which is charged with the maintenance

of law and order and protection of life and property within the respective jurisdiction.
2. The California Highway Patrol will coordinate and control all traffic on the highways over which it has traffic control jurisdiction.

B. Operational areas

In each operational area there shall be a law enforcement coordinator selected in accordance with procedure established by the operational area officials concerned. He shall be the sheriff of the operational area or a chief of police of a city within the area.

C. Region

1. In each region there shall be a law enforcement coordinator who shall be an experienced law enforcement officer. He shall be selected by a majority vote of the operational area law enforcement coordinators within the region.
2. In each region there shall be a law enforcement coordinating center within the State's regional center; it shall be equipped to perform its emergency function.

D. State

1. Prior to a state of extreme emergency, the Chief, Law Enforcement Division, California Disaster Office, will be responsible for administrative action and coordination necessary to develop the civil defense law enforcement program.
2. Upon the existence of a state of extreme emergency proclaimed by the Governor, the Attorney General, in accordance with provisions of Administrative Order No. 61-1 as approved by the Governor, is responsible for state law enforcement coordination.

VII. OPERATIONS

A. Local

Chiefs of police and sheriffs shall act in the following capacity:

1. Establish and maintain liaison with the operational area law enforcement coordinator, and through him with the regional law enforcement coordinator, in order to relate local plans to State plans for law enforcement civil defense and disaster services.
2. Develop and implement local plans and procedures to facilitate effective law enforcement participation in disaster and civil defense operations.
3. Establish liaison with local Commanders of the California Highway Patrol for the purpose of coordination and the development of law enforcement assistance plans.
4. Advise the local defense director on law enforcement matters.

5. Assist the Law Enforcement Division of the California Disaster Office in compiling and maintaining lists of special law enforcement equipment and specially trained personnel, to include strength of regular and auxiliary or reserve personnel. Copies of these lists will be sent by the Law Enforcement Division to chiefs of police and sheriffs as soon as compiled and corrected and at least annually thereafter.
6. Request law enforcement mutual aid from other jurisdictions and agencies in accordance with established procedures.
7. Establish liaison with local units of the California National Guard to facilitate use of military resources in disasters and emergencies.
8. Establish procedures to insure the rapid flow of information concerning riots, civil disturbances, or other law enforcement problems of major consequence, to the law enforcement operational area coordinator.

Chiefs of police and sheriffs should integrate special disaster and civil defense functions into the normal functions of their respective departments. These will generally include the following:

1. Administration
    a. Direction, supervision, and coordination of all essential law enforcement disaster and civil defense operations.
    b. Determination and assignment of responsibility, authority, and liability of reserve or auxiliary personnel.
    c. Liaison with appropriate authorities concerning disaster and civil defense problems and additional resources. These include, but are not limited to the following:
    Law Enforcement Division, California Disaster Office.
    Federal Bureau of Investigation.
    United States Defense Forces.
    Fire Services.
    California Highway Patrol.
    California National Guard.
    State agencies having law enforcement responsibilities within their jurisdiction.
2. Procurement and supply
    a. Procurement, storage, and issue of equipment used in law enforcement operations. (Arrangements should be made to obtain standby or duplicate equipment and special equipment not ordinarily used.)
    b. Establish procedures to obtain additional and special equipment from state agency resources.

3. Records and identification
    a. Identification of disaster casualties and found property will require coordination of efforts and information from mortuaries, public health officials, dentists, the State Division of Criminal Identification and Investigation, the Federal Bureau of Investigation, and other agencies.
    b. Liaison should be established with Welfare Services, Red Cross, and State Division of Criminal Identification and Investigation.
    c. Procedures for the fingerprinting, photographing, and clearance through both the State Division of Criminal Identification and Investigation and the Federal Bureau of Investigation.
    d. Issuance of passes and permits should be established.
4. Communications
    a. Provisions should be made for expansion of law enforcement communications facilities, including alternate communications facilities and messenger service. Insofar as possible, law enforcement communications facilities should be reserved for exclusive law enforcement use. To insure continuous communications standby power should be provided.
    b. Plans and procedures should be established for communications between the law enforcement agency and appropriate civil defense coordinators.
    c. Equipment should be acquired for use on the State Emergency Net and Inter-City Law Net.
5. Transportation
    a. Provisions should be made for adequate mobility to meet emergency situations. Law enforcement vehicles should be restricted to law enforcement functions.
    b. Determination should be made as to the adequacy of present equipment and provision made for procurement of any additional equipment needed.
6. Detention
    a. Plans should be made for expanded and alternate jail facilities.
    b. Inventories of detention facilities, including the number, type, capacity, food service, etc., should be made and maintained in a current status.
7. Patrol
    a. Arrangements for necessary expansion of number and distribution of patrol force should be made, including use of supplemental law enforcement mutual aid personnel and/or military personnel.
    b. Special functional details within the patrol force, including unexploded bomb reconnaissance, radiological defense, chemi-

cal defense duties, and prevention of sabotage should be prepared.
8. Traffic
   a. Plan for the control of vehicular and pedestrian traffic under emergency conditions.
   b. Prepare plans for the establishment of enforcement of traffic priority and dispatch systems.
   c. Coordinate interjurisdictional traffic movement with the California Highway Patrol. The California Highway Patrol, through its established State, Zone and Area Traffic Control Centers, will control and coordinate all traffic on the road systems over which it has traffic control jurisdiction.
9. Criminal investigation
   a. Cooperate with proper authorities in the prevention of sabotage, espionage, and subversive activities.
   b. Cooperate with the military services in matters concerning their areas of responsibilities.
10. Vice control
    a. Provide for control of alcoholic beverages and narcotics. Coordinate with state and federal agencies concerned, i.e., State Division of Narcotic Enforcement, State Board of Equalization, Federal Bureau of Narcotics, and the Federal Alcoholic Tax Unit.
11. Information
    a. Provide for the collection, evaluation, and dissemination of operational information and official regulations and orders to higher and lower echelons.
    b. Make every effort to advise the Operational Area and Regional Law Enforcement Coordinators and the Law Enforcement Division of the California Disaster Office of a situation which may be beyond the capability of the local agency.
12. Specialized operations
    a. Plan for support by office and utility company personnel in riot areas, sniper suppression, crowd control, and riot suppression and prevention.
    b. Provide security for police building and essential communications facilities.

B. Operational Areas

Operational Area Law Enforcement Coordinators should act in the following capacity:
1. Establish and maintain an effective law enforcement coordinating center and such alternate centers as are deemed necessary.

2. Maintain lists of special law enforcement equipment and specially trained personnel and the number of regular and auxiliary or reserve personnel within the operational area.
3. Insure that full and complete information relating to riots, civil disturbances, and other major law enforcement problems is gathered from within the operational area and furnished to the Regional Law Enforcement Coordinator.
4. During a state of extreme emergency:
   a. Perform assigned law enforcement functions.
   b. Provide the necessary law enforcement representation at the operational area civil defense emergency operating center if the latter is in a facility separate from the law enforcement coordinating center.

C. Regions

Regional Law Enforcement Coordinators should act in the following capacity:

1. Establish and maintain an effective regional law enforcement coordinating center and such alternate centers as are deemed necessary.
2. Maintain lists of special law enforcement equipment and specially trained personnel and the strength of regular and auxiliary or reserve personnel of the law enforcement agencies within the region.
3. Initiate contact with law enforcement administrators within the region to assist in collection of intelligence and information relating to major law enforcement activities (riots, civil disturbances, etc.), utilize the information to assist in planning for use of regional law enforcement resources and furnish the information and planning to the Law Enforcement Division.
4. During a state of extreme emergency, disaster, or local peril:
   a. Perform assigned law enforcement functions.
   b. Provide the necessary law enforcement representation at the regional emergency operating center, if the latter is in a facility separate from the law enforcement coordinating center.

D. State Level

The Law Enforcement Division of the California Disaster Office shall act in the following capacity:

1. Coordinate, integrate, and implement law enforcement planning, and activities for use of mutual aid and state resources.
2. Maintain lists of special law enforcement equipment, specially trained personnel, and all regular and auxiliary or reserve law enforcement personnel and equipment within the state.

3. Organize, direct, and supervise the law enforcement services of the California Disaster Office and correlate its activities with other Divisions of the California Disaster Office.
4. Coordinate and implement the gathering and collection of information and intelligence relating to possible requirements for Law Enforcement Mutual Aid or for assistance from state agencies to support local law enforcement agencies in local peril, disaster, or emergency which may arise out of civil disturbances, demonstrations, or riots, and provide this information to the Executive Branch of State Government.
5. Advise the Director of the California Disaster Office and members of his staff on law enforcement matters.
6. Maintain liaison with the Commissioner of the California Highway Patrol, in order to coordinate and integrate plans for traffic control and the participation of the Department in the law enforcement operation.
7. Maintain liaison with the Governor's Law Enforcement Advisory Committee, federal and state departments and agencies, and local law enforcement officials, in order to achieve close coordination and cooperation in planning and operations in civil defense activities.
8. Facilitate the flow of law enforcement information from federal and state organizations to regional, operational area, and local law enforcement officials.
9. Maintain law enforcement emergency equipment vans and provide equipment, upon request, to departments in need of specialized equipment.
10. Maintain law enforcement communications vans and facilitate their availability to jurisdictions requiring supplemented law enforcement mutual aid communications.
11. Maintain liaison with the Attorney General's representative in order to keep the Attorney General informed of changes in law enforcement civil defense plans and regulations, mutual aid agreements, and current developments in all disaster situations.

MILITARY AND VETERANS CODE

Chapter 1, Division 7, Military and Veterans Code, added at the 1943 First Extraordinary Session, as amended effective September 20, 1963.

Article 1. General Provisions

1501. As used in this chapter, "state of extreme emergency" means the duly proclaimed existence of conditions of extreme peril to the safety of persons and property within the State caused by an enemy attack or threatened attack by land, sea, or air, or when upon the advice of the commanding general of this area, such an attack is imminent, an air raid alarm, sabotage, or other cause such as air pollution, fire, flood, storm, epidemic, riot or earthquake, which conditions by reason of their magnitude are or are likely to be beyond the control of the services, personnel, equipment and facilities of any single county, city and county, or city and require the combined forces of a "mutual aid region or regions" to combat. "State of extreme emergency" does not include nor does any provision of this chapter apply to any condition resulting from a labor controversy.

As used in this chapter, "state of disaster" means the duly proclaimed existence of conditions of extreme peril to the safety of persons and property within the State caused by such conditions as air pollution, fire, flood, storm, epidemic, riot or earthquake, or other conditions except as a result of war-caused disaster, which conditions, by reason of their magnitude, are or are likely to be beyond the control of the services, personnel, equipment and facilities of any single county, city and county, or city and require the combined forces of a mutual aid region or regions to combat. "State of disaster" does not include nor does any provision of this chapter apply to any condition resulting from a labor controversy.

As used in this chapter "local peril," "local emergency" or "local disaster" shall mean the existence of conditions, within the territorial limits of a local agency in the absence of a duly proclaimed state of extreme emergency or state of disaster, which conditions are a result of an emergency created by great public calamity such as extraordinary fire, flood, storm, epidemic, earthquake or other disaster which is, or is likely to be, beyond the control of the services, personnel, equipment and facilities of that agency and require the combined forces of other local agencies to combat. (Stats. 1943 1st Ex. Sess., Ch. 1, as amended by Stats. 1959, Ch. 1330).

MUTUAL AID REGIONS
STATE of CALIFORNIA

B
A MUTUAL AID AGREEMENT

Some jurisdictions are involved with formal mutual aid agreements which clarify the scope and extent of their cooperation. Presented here is an example of an agreement between jurisdictions and a master agreement between the State and other subordinate jurisdictions.

This agreement made and entered into by and between the State of _____, its various departments and agencies, and the various political subdivisions, municipal corporations, and other public agencies of the State of _____

WITNESSETH:

Whereas, it is necessary that all of the resources and facilities of the State, its various departments and agencies, and all its political subdivisions, municipal corporations, and other public agencies be made available to prevent and combat the effect of disasters which may result from such calamities as flood, fire, earthquake, pestilence, war, sabotage, and riot; and

Whereas, it is desirable that each of the parties hereto should voluntarily aid and assist each other in the event that a disaster should occur, by the interchange of services and facilities, including, but not limited to, fire, police, medical and health, communication, and transportation services and facilities, to cope with the problems of rescue, relief, evacuation, rehabilitation, and reconstruction which would arise in the event of a disaster; and

Whereas, it is necessary and desirable that a cooperative agreement be executed for the interchange of such mutual aid on a local, county-wide, regional, statewide, and interstate basis;

Now, therefore, it is hereby agreed by and between each and all of the parties hereto as follows:

1. Each party shall develop a plan providing for the effective mobilization of all its resources and facilities, both public and private, to cope with any type of disaster.

2. Each party agrees to furnish resources and facilities and to render services to each and every other party to this agreement to prevent and combat any type of disaster in accordance with duly adopted mutual aid opera-

tional plans, whether heretofore or hereafter adopted, detailing the method and manner by which such resources, facilities, and services are to be made available and furnished, which operational plans may include provisions for training and testing to make such mutual aid effective; provided, however, that no party shall be required to deplete unreasonably its own resources, facilities, and services in furnishing such mutual aid.

3. It is expressly understood that this agreement and the operational plans adopted pursuant thereto shall not supplant existing agreements between some of the parties hereto providing for the exchange or furnishing of certain types of facilities and services on a reimbursable, exchange, or other basis, but that the mutual aid extended under this agreement and the operational plans adopted pursuant thereto, shall be without reimbursement unless otherwise expressly provided for by the parties to this agreement or as provided _____, _____; and that such mutual aid is intended to be available in the event of a disaster of such magnitude that it is, or is likely to be, beyond the control of a single party and requires the combined forces of several or all of the parties to this agreement to combat.

4. It is expressly understood that the mutual aid extended under this agreement and the operational plans adopted pursuant thereto shall be available and furnished in all cases of local peril or emergency and in all cases in which a State of Extreme Emergency has been proclaimed.

5. It is expressly understood that any mutual aid extended under this agreement and the operational plans adopted pursuant thereto, is furnished in accordance with the _____ and other applicable provisions of law, and except as otherwise provided by law that: "The responsible local official in whose jurisdiction an incident requiring mutual aid has occurred shall remain in charge at such incident including the direction of such personnel and equipment provided him through the operation of such mutual aid plans."

6. It is expressly understood that when and as the State of _____ enters into mutual aid agreements with other states and the Federal Government that the parties to this agreement shall abide by such mutual aid agreements in accordance with the law.

7. Upon approval or execution of this agreement by the parties hereto all mutual aid operational plans heretofore approved by the State _____, or its predecessors, and in effect as to some of the parties hereto, shall remain in full force and effect as to them until the same may be amended, revised, or modified. Additional mutual aid operational plans and amendments, revisions, or modifications of existing or hereafter adopted mutual aid operational plans, shall be adopted as follows:

(a) County-wide and local mutual aid operational plans shall be developed by the parties thereto and are operative as between the parties thereto in accordance with the provisions of such operational plans. Such operational plans shall be submitted to the State _____ for approval. The State _____ shall notify each party to such operational plans of its approval, and shall also send copies of such operational plans to other parties to this agreement who did not participate in such operational plans and who are in the same area and affected by such operational plans. Such operational plans shall be operative as to such other parties twenty days after receipt thereof unless within that time the party by resolution or notice given to the State _____, in the same manner as notice of termination of participation in this agreement, declines to participate in the particular operational plan.

(b) State-wide and regional mutual aid operational plans shall be approved by the State _____ and copies thereof shall forthwith be sent to each and every party affected by such operational plans. Such operational plans shall be operative as to the parties affected thereby twenty days after receipt thereof unless within that time the party by resolution or notice given to the State _____, in the same manner as notice of termination of participation in this agreement, declines to participate in the particular operational plan.

(c) The declination of one or more of the parties to participate in a particular operational plan or any amendment, revision, or modification thereof, shall not affect the operation of this agreement and the other operational plans adopted pursuant thereto.

(d) Any party may at any time by resolution or notice given to the State _____, in the same manner as notice of termination of participation in this agreement, decline to participate in any particular operational plan, which declination shall become effective twenty days after filing with the State _____.

(e) The State _____ shall send copies of all operational plans to those state departments and agencies designated by the Governor. The Governor may upon behalf of any department or agency give notice that such department or agency declines to participate in a particular operational plan.

(f) The State _____, in sending copies of operational plans and other notices and information to the parties to this agreement, shall send copies to the Governor and any department or agency head designated by him; the chairman of the board of supervisors, the clerk of the board of supervisors, and any other officer designated by a county; the mayor, the clerk of the city council, and any other officer designated by a city; the executive head, the clerk of the governing body, or other officer of other political subdivisions and public agencies as designated by such parties.

8. This agreement shall become effective as to each party when approved or executed by the party, and shall remain operative and effective as between each and every party that has heretofore or hereafter approved or executed this agreement, until participation in this agreement is terminated by the

party. The termination by one or more of the parties of its participation in this agreement shall not affect the operation of this agreement as between the other parties thereto. Upon approval or execution of this agreement the State _____ shall send copies of all approved and existing mutual aid operational plans affecting such party which shall become operative as to such party twenty days after receipt thereof unless within that time the party by resolution or notice given to the State _____, in the same manner as notice of termination of participation in this agreement, declines to participate in any particular operational plan. The State _____ shall keep every party currently advised of who the other parties to this agreement are and whether any of them has declined to participate in any particular operational plan.

9. Approval or execution of this agreement shall be as follows:

(a) The Governor shall execute a copy of this agreement on behalf of the State of _____ and the various departments and agencies thereof. Upon execution by the Governor a signed copy shall forthwith be filed with the State _____.

(b) Counties, cities, and other political subdivisions and public agencies having no legislative or governing body shall execute a copy of this agreement and forthwith file a signed copy with the State _____.

10. Termination of participation in this agreement may be effected by any party as follows:

(a) The Governor upon behalf of the State and its various department and agencies, and the executive head of those political subdivisions and public agencies having no legislative or governing body, shall file a written notice of termination of participation in this agreement with the State _____ and this agreement is terminated as to such party twenty days after the filing of such notice.

(b) Counties, cities, and other political subdivisions and public agencies having a legislative or governing body shall by resolution give notice of termination of participation in this agreement and file a certified copy of such resolution with the State _____, and this agreement is terminated as to such party twenty days after the filing of such resolution.

In Witness Whereof this agreement has been executed and approved and is effective and operative as to each of the parties as herein provided.

(Seal)

(Governor)
Signed: _____

On behalf of the State of _____ and all its Departments and Agencies

(Secretary of State)
Attest: _____

MUTUAL AID AND JOINT POWERS AGREEMENT

This Agreement made and entered into by and between the participant municipal corporations and political subdivisions of _____, _____, _____, _____, _____, located within operational area _____ of the Civil Defense Region _____ of the State of _____, which now or hereafter become signatories hereto;

WITNESSETH:

Whereas, it is necessary and desirable that the resources, personnel, equipment and facilities of any one party to this agreement be made available to any other party to prevent, combat, or eliminate a probable, imminent, or actual threat to life or property resulting from a local peril, local emergency, local disaster, or civil disturbance, in the absence of a duly proclaimed "state of extreme emergency" or "state of disaster," and to render mutual and supplementary police protection one to the other as the need may arise; and

Whereas, extensive loss of life and property may be precluded by the immediate and adequate response of the forces of local government to what are or may be disturbances and disasters; and

Whereas, the parties signatory to this agreement are all located within the operational Area _____ of the Civil Defense Region _____ of the State of _____, or have assigned responsibilities within the Area, and therefore, have mutual interests and objectives to accomplish with reference to the preservation and protection of life and property within said area; and

Whereas, the parties signatory to this agreement are all respectively public agencies with the powers to provide for common defense, and the power to act in case of emergency or disaster are all powers common to the parties signatory hereto; and

Whereas, under the provisions of the _____ Code of the State of _____, "The legislative body of any local agency may contract with any other local agency for the furnishing of supplementary fire or police protection to such other local agency," such statute having been interpreted that a general law city may agree or contract with other cities to render mutual police protection; and pursuant to the _____ Code, Joint Powers Agreements; and other laws of the State of _____, power is given to each of the parties to this agreement to so contract; and

Whereas, it is expressly understood that this agreement and the operation orders adopted pursuant thereto shall not supplant existing agreements between some of the parties hereto providing for the exchange or furnishing of certain types of facilities and services on a reimbursable exchange or other basis, nor to supplant the mandatory agreements required by law in the event of a duly proclaimed emergency; however, it is the intent to supplement any or all agreements now in effect between or among the parties hereto for the purpose of providing mutual aid.

Now, therefore, it is hereby agreed by and between each and all of the parties hereto as follows:

1. Each public agency signatory hereto agrees to furnish supplementary police protection to the other public agencies signatory to this agreement in the event of local peril, local emergency, local disaster, civil disturbance and such other occasions as the need may arise, and authority is hereby given to the police officers of all signatory public agencies by and between each to enforce all laws and take all police action in cases involving the safety of life or property.

2. It further is covenanted and agreed by and between the parties hereto that when a police agency of any of the signatory cities has knowledge or information pertaining to an incident necessitating police action or law enforcement within the jurisdiction of another city, that the police agency of the city so acquiring said information immediately shall notify the police agency in which the incident arose or occurred, and then shall have authority to proceed to the scene of the incident and upon arriving at the scene of the incident may exercise jurisdiction of the occurrence to its conclusion.

3. Each party signatory hereto shall develop a plan providing for the effective mobilization of its police resources, and the strategy and tactics to be employed in the maintenance of peace and order, such plan to be made available to the Chiefs of the respective police department. Such other plans and operation orders as may be necessary to effectuate the purpose of this agreement are authorized to be made by the respective rsponsible local officials.

4. The mutual aid extended under this agreement and the operation orders adopted pursuant to this agreement shall be without reimbursement unless otherwise expressly provided for by the parties to this agreement or as provided by law in the event of a duly proclaimed state of extreme emergency or state of disaster, it being understood that the respective covenants contained in this agreement shall constitute the sole consideration for such services. Provided further that each party hereto shall maintain a record of direct costs of labor and material furnished pursuant to this agreement.

5. The responsible local official in whose jurisdiction an incident requiring mutual aid has occurred, unless otherwise provided, shall remain in charge at such incident including the direction of such personnel and equipment provided him through the operation of such mutual aid plan.

6. It is mutually understood and agreed that nothing contained in this agreement shall require or relieve any party hereto from the necessity and obligation of furnishing adequate protection to life and property within their own areas and no party shall be required to deplete unreasonably his own resources, facilities, and services in furnishing such mutual aid.

7. Any services performed or expenditures made in connection with the furnishing of assistance shall conclusively be presumed to be for the direct protection of the inhabitants and property of the party furnishing the assistance and for the direct benefit of all inhabitants of the area.

8. This agreement shall not be construed as, or deemed to be an agreement for the benefit of any third party or parties, and no third party or parties shall have the right of action hereunder for any cause whatsoever.

9. It is the intent of this agreement that the employee or the public entity by which he is employed has the same privileges, benefits, rights, immunities and liabilities while rendering extra-territorial aid as when rendering services within the territorial limits of their particular jurisdiction. Provided, further, in the event that the responding party is named as a co-defendant or otherwise exposed to liability or claim because of the acts or omissions of the employees or supervisory personnel of the requesting party, then and in that event the requesting party shall indemnify the responding party for such damage, including but not limited to defense costs, as may be occasioned by the responding party.

10. The declination of one or more of the parties to participate in this agreement and operation orders or any amendment, revision, or modification thereof, shall not affect the operation of this agreement and operation orders adopted pursuant thereto insofar as the validity of the agreement pertains to the signatory parties.

11. This agreement shall become effective as to each party when approved or executed by the party, and shall remain operative and effective as between each and every party that has heretofore or hereafter approved or executed this agreement, until participation in this agreement is terminated by the party. The termination by one or more of the parties of its participation in this agreement shall not affect the operation of this agreement as between the other parties thereto.

12. Approval or execution of this agreement shall be by resolution of the legislative body of the parties hereto approving and agreeing to abide by this agreement entitled Mutual Aid and Joint Powers Agreement. Upon adoption of such a resolution, certified copy thereof shall forthwith be filed with the Clerk of the public agencies a party thereto.

13. Termination of participation in this agreement may be effected by any party by a resolution of the legislative body of said public agency giving notice of termination of participation in this agreement to the Clerk of

the cities of public agencies a party hereto and this agreement is terminated as to such party twenty days after the filing of such resolution.

In witness whereof this agreement has been executed and approved and is effective and operative as to each of the parties as herein provided.

City of _____

Mayor

Attest:

City Clerk
(Seal)

C
MODEL ORGANIZATION AND FUNCTION PLAN

This is an example of a partial "Organization and Function" plan which shows changes in responsibility for organizational units during progressive periods of a disaster. Although the plan is outdated, it is nonetheless a good example of changes in unit responsibilities as disaster control is achieved.

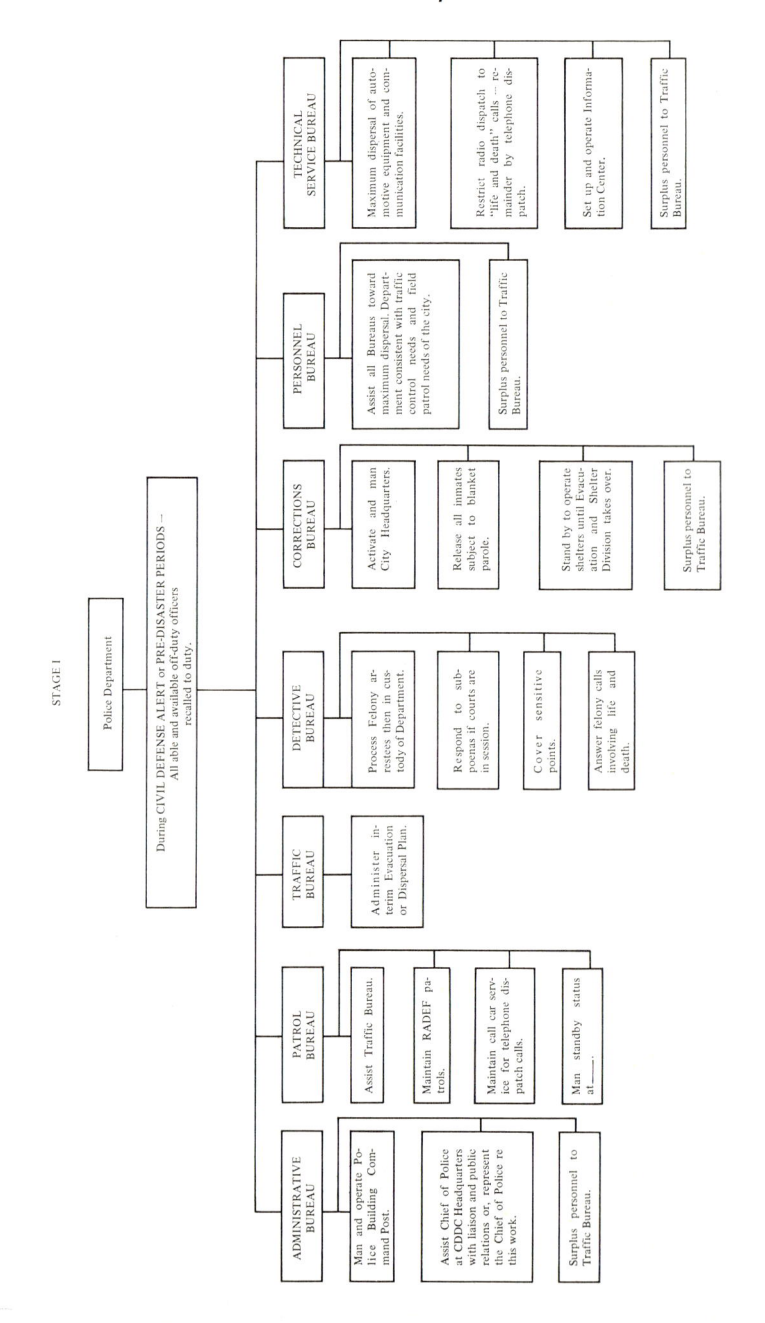

Police Disaster Operations

STAGE I

Police Department

During CIVIL DEFENSE ALERT or PRE-DISASTER PERIODS — All able and available off-duty officers recalled to duty.

ADMINISTRATIVE BUREAU
- Man and operate Police Building Command Post.
- Assist Chief of Police at CDDC Headquarters with liaison and public relations or, represent the Chief of Police re this work.
- Surplus personnel to Traffic Bureau.

PATROL BUREAU
- Assist Traffic Bureau.
- Maintain RADEF patrols.
- Maintain call car service for telephone dispatch calls.
- Man standby status at ____.

TRAFFIC BUREAU
- Administer interim Evacuation or Dispersal Plan.

DETECTIVE BUREAU
- Process Felony arrestees then in custody of Department.
- Respond to subpoenas if courts are in session.
- Cover sensitive points.
- Answer felony calls involving life and death.

CORRECTIONS BUREAU
- Activate and man City Headquarters.
- Release all inmates subject to blanket parole.
- Stand by to operate shelters until Evacuation and Shelter Division takes over.
- Surplus personnel to Traffic Bureau.

PERSONNEL BUREAU
- Assist all Bureaus toward maximum dispersal. Deployment consistent with traffic control needs and field patrol needs of the city.
- Surplus personnel to Traffic Bureau.

TECHNICAL SERVICE BUREAU
- Maximum dispersal of automotive equipment and communication facilities.
- Restrict radio dispatch to "life and death" calls — remainder by telephone dispatch.
- Set up and operate Information Center.
- Surplus personnel to Traffic Bureau.

Model Organization and Function Plan

STAGE II

Police Department

During NORMALIZATION PERIODS
(Emphasis upon relieving human hardships)

ADMINISTRATIVE BUREAU
- Assist Chief of Police with liaison and public relations at Civil Defense and Disaster Headquarters.

PATROL BUREAU
- Report damage.
- Report RADEF if involved.
- Establish and administer police needs of Theater and Remainder.
- Establish and operate Theater Command Post.

TRAFFIC BUREAU
- Establish and administer Traffic Line as needed by Theater Command.
- Maintain motorcycle patrols in Theater — Remainder only if requested by Patrol Bureau.

DETECTIVE BUREAU
- Life and death investigations in Theater — Traffic Line — Remainder.
- Defer all others until Rehab. Period.
- Court work as subpoenaed.

CORRECTIONS BUREAU
- Operate auxiliary City Headquarters if needed.
- Operate shelters as needed until Evacuation and Shelter Division takes over.

PERSONNEL BUREAU
- Balance man-power in terms of need and availability.
- Administer mutual aid — mobile support — military assistance as required by Chief of Police.
- Administer auxiliary police enrollment program.

TECHNICAL SERVICES BUREAU
- Adapt Communications — Supply — Equipment — Maintenance — Records — Property to situation and provide best available in the circumstances.

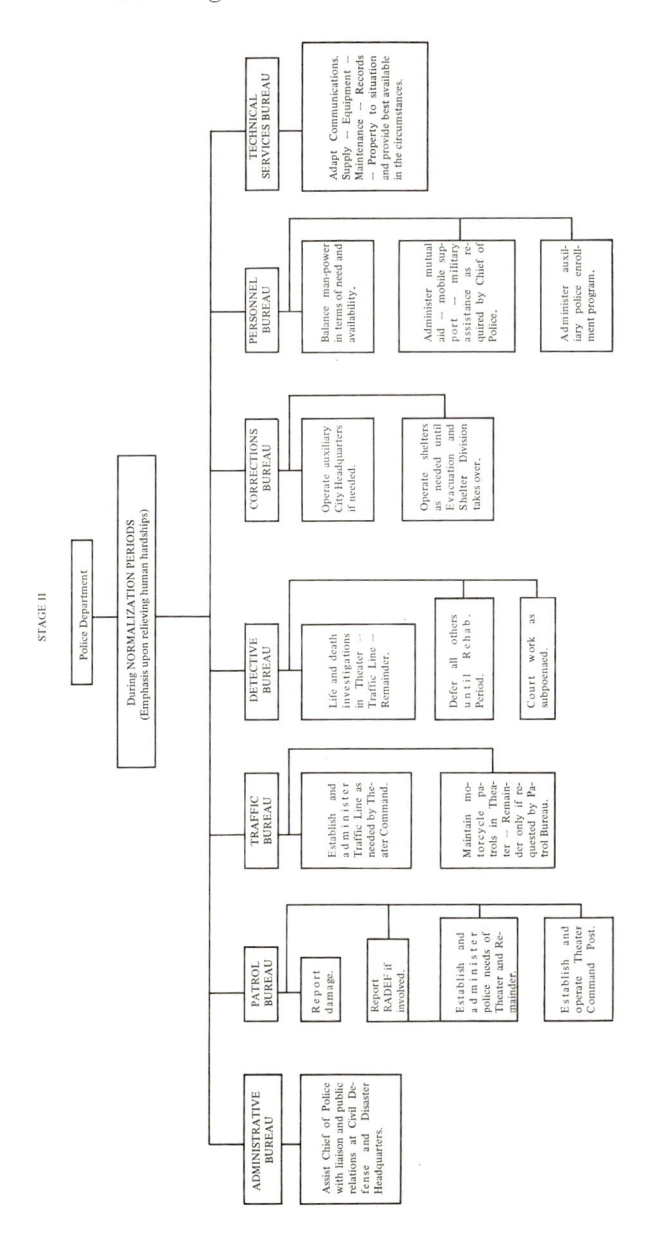

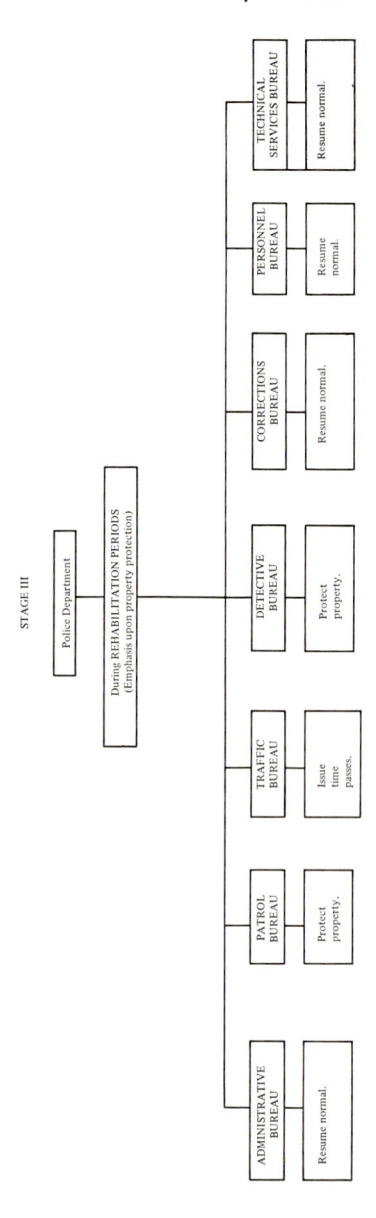

STAGE III

Police Department

During REHABILITATION PERIODS
(Emphasis upon property protection)

- **ADMINISTRATIVE BUREAU** — Resume normal.
- **PATROL BUREAU** — Protect property.
- **TRAFFIC BUREAU** — Issue time passes.
- **DETECTIVE BUREAU** — Protect property.
- **CORRECTIONS BUREAU** — Resume normal.
- **PERSONNEL BUREAU** — Resume normal.
- **TECHNICAL SERVICES BUREAU** — Resume normal.

D
PLAN FOR CHANGE OF FUNCTION DURING A DISASTER

Another example of planning for change of function during a disaster compares routine organizational structure with disaster structure in a medium-sized police department.

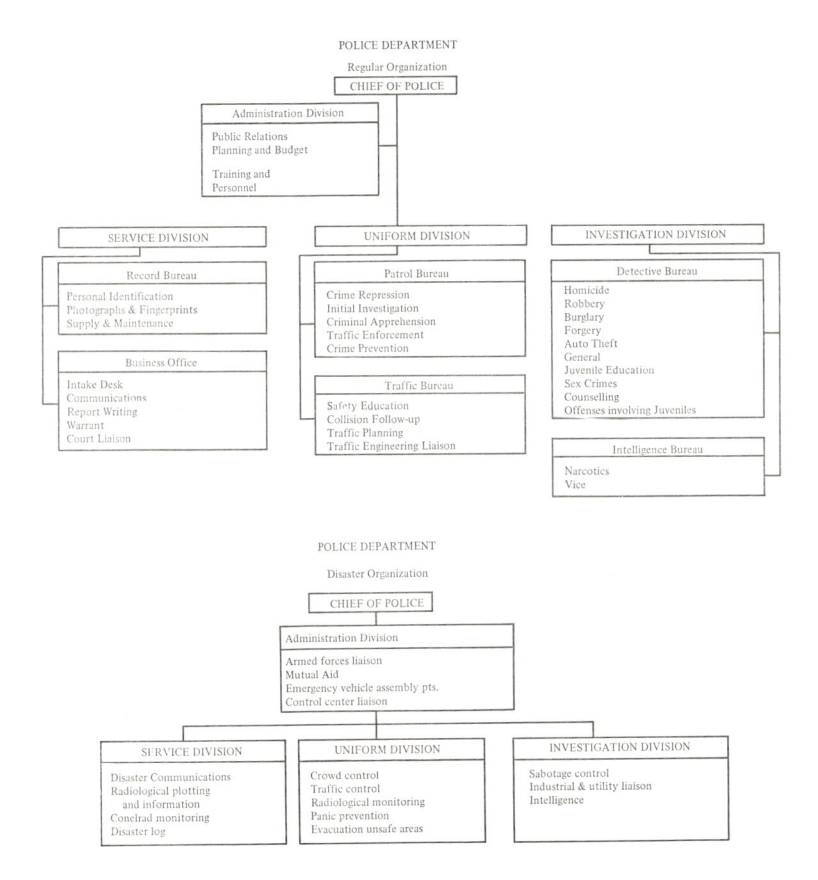

POLICE DEPARTMENT
Regular Organization

CHIEF OF POLICE

Administration Division
- Public Relations
- Planning and Budget
- Training and Personnel

SERVICE DIVISION

Record Bureau
- Personal Identification
- Photographs & Fingerprints
- Supply & Maintenance

Business Office
- Intake Desk
- Communications
- Report Writing
- Warrant
- Court Liaison

UNIFORM DIVISION

Patrol Bureau
- Crime Repression
- Initial Investigation
- Criminal Apprehension
- Traffic Enforcement
- Crime Prevention

Traffic Bureau
- Safety Education
- Collision Follow-up
- Traffic Planning
- Traffic Engineering Liaison

INVESTIGATION DIVISION

Detective Bureau
- Homicide
- Robbery
- Burglary
- Forgery
- Auto Theft
- General
- Juvenile Education
- Sex Crimes
- Counselling
- Offenses involving Juveniles

Intelligence Bureau
- Narcotics
- Vice

POLICE DEPARTMENT
Disaster Organization

CHIEF OF POLICE

Administration Division
- Armed forces liaison
- Mutual Aid
- Emergency vehicle assembly pts.
- Control center liaison

SERVICE DIVISION
- Disaster Communications
- Radiological plotting and information
- Conelrad monitoring
- Disaster log

UNIFORM DIVISION
- Crowd control
- Traffic control
- Radiological monitoring
- Panic prevention
- Evacuation unsafe areas

INVESTIGATION DIVISION
- Sabotage control
- Industrial & utility liaison
- Intelligence

E
SIMULATION GAMES

A research report on simulation games by Sergeant William M. Fincke, Pasadena Police Department. The report defines terms, presents principles, and illustrates an application of simulation gaming to disaster training.

Controlling purpose: To acquaint members of the Independent Study Simulation Group with the general principles of simulation games.

    I. Definitions.
        A. Definitions of terms used in simulation games.

   II. Simulation games.
        A. Simulation games are more than a physical training device.
        B. Educational games use simulation techniques.
        C. The major areas of penetration.
        D. The trends in simulation games.
        E. The major objectives in simulation games.
        F. Simulation games have passed through several stages.
        G. The basic forms of simulation.

  III. Elementary simulation design.
        A. Selection of objectives.
        B. System analysis.
        C. Sequential analysis.
        D. Decision analysis.
        E. The model.
        F. Refining the model.
        G. The critique.

I. DEFINITIONS

Simulation: An act or process of simulating the central features of reality.[1]

Games: An entertainment and/or educational device which uses some form of simulation.[2]

Simulation Game: A combined teaching and research technique using simulation and gaming techniques to achieve a real life situation game without real life consequences.[3]

Simulator: A person, object or device which simulates the central features of reality.[4]

Symbolic Simulation: A form of simulation exercise where all aspects are reduced to symbols. These symbols are then played against a previously programmed computer.[5]

Operational Simulation: A form of simulation exercise, using humans, which is primarily used to test the adequacy of ongoing systems and train their respective staff members.[6]

Input: All information presented to the senses of the players in a simulation exercise.[7]

In Basket (In Tray) Method: A communication technique where all input is received by the player through his "in basket" in the form of written messages.[8]

Output: All actions on the part of the players as a result of the input received by them.[9]

Feedback: Information returned to the players concerning the actual results of their output.

---

[1] Harold S. Guetzhow: *Simulation in International Relations.* Richard C. Snyder, Ed., p. 25.
[2] Sarane S. Boocock and E. O. Schild: *Simulation Games in Learning.* p. 14.
[3] *Ibid.*, p. 55.
[4] *Emergency Operations Simulation Training, Simulation Manual.* p. 1.
[5] Terence P. Harney: *Simulation Application for Disaster Command and Control.* p. 2.
[6] *Ibid.*
[7] Boocock and Schild: *op. cit.*, pp. 75-76.
[8] *E.O.S.T. Operations Manual*, pp. 37-39.
[9] Boocock and Schild: *loc. cit.*

Replications: The physical facility (mock-up) which includes the necessary job aids to conduct a simulation exercise.[10]

Scenario: A chronological description of the significant events that are to take place during the simulation exercise.[11]

II. SIMULATION GAMES

Most of us think of simulation as being associated with a physical device such as the Apollo simulator or a baby's pacifier. We also think of games as being strictly entertaining rather than educational. Today this is not the case. Simulation exercises have incorporated many of the techniques commonly found in gaming. Gaming has also been used as an educational device in many levels of education and no longer should be considered as being strictly entertaining. Gaming has also incorporated many of the techniques used in simulation. Today it is difficult to separate simulation from gaming and in most cases the two are used interchangeably.

Games are as old as man and usually their basic objective has been entertainment. The educational game aims at learning with the major difference being the degree to which the game approaches reality and the degree which the players exercise judgment and skill in determining the outcome of the game as opposed to luck.[1]

Simulation for our purposes can be defined as an actor process of simulating the central features of reality and may or may not incorporate the use of a simulation device per se.[2] Simulation games have been used as a vehicle for research and training for many years. The major areas of penetration have been in business decision-making, bargaining, diplomatic and war games, man-

---

[10]Harney: *op. cit.*, p. 4.
[11]*Ibid.*
[1]G. R. Andlinger: Business Games—Play One, *Harvard Business Review*. 36.2 (March-April, 1958), p. 117.
[2]H. S. Guetzhow: *Simulation in International Relations*. R. C. Snyder, Ed., p. 25.

machine systems, higher mental processes, community conflict and emergency operations.[3]

There are three major trends in the use of simulation. The first is the use of human subjects under quasi-laboratory conditions to create replicas of complex organizational systems and/or social processes. The second is the use of human subjects in a non-laboratory but contrived setting to create replicas as mentioned above. The third trend is in the use of machines to experimentally simulate mental and social systems. It is also used to experimentally simulate the operation of certain mechanical devices. In the main, simulation may be divided into two major areas with regard to objectives. The first area is research-theory building and the second area is education. There are three basic applications for simulation in the first area. The first is the use of simulation to test areas where there is insufficient data to confirm a specific theory or process. The second is the use of simulation to gain relatively quick insight into novel problems which have no apparent counterpart in prior experience. The third is the use of simulation to study complex communications networks in organizations by simulating smaller counterparts.

In these areas the techniques used in simulation exercises give the operator the advantage of allowing him to see the operation as it unfolds under circumstances which allow him to penetrate portions of the system which seemed hopelessly complex before.[4] Simulation also aids in uncovering information gaps, identifies redundancies, indicates the systems capacity under varying loads, identifies resource deficiencies, develops strategies for use of limited resources and allows for advance changes in plans.[5] In addition this type of simulation allows one to examine hard-to-solve problems, identifies critical needs, and develops interaction skills. It also has a high safety factor, a low relative cost, is controllable, and allows for repetition.[6]

---

[3]Richard C. Snyder: *Simulation in International Relations.* p. 3.
[4]Richard C. Snyder: *Simulation in International Relations.* pp. 3-4.
[5]Terence P. Harney: *Simulation Application for Disaster Command and Control.* p. 8.
[6]*Ibid.,* p. 10.

The second major area is education. This area consists of initial and recurrent education or training.[7] There has been a lot of controversy over whether educational simulation actually teaches and if so, how. Educational simulation has passed through two stages of controversy over the years and is presently going through a third. The first stage is referred to as "The Acceptance of Faith Period." During this stage, prior to 1963, there was much enthusiasm about educational simulation with little concern for collecting evidence to support the general conclusions.

The second stage is referred to as "The Post Honeymoon Period" and lasted from 1963 through 1965. During this stage researchers attempted to hold controlled experiments with simulation games used in education. Generally inconclusive results led to sobering conclusions that educational simulation games were not the solution for the many ills in education, that simulation games had serious flaws and that instruments set up to measure particular simulation games were not adequate to successfully measure the results in question.

During the present stage referred to as "Realistic Optimism" the feeling is that education simulation games do teach, that they are worthwhile, however, more research is needed to determine why.[8]

Generally a new technology is preceded by scientific knowledge. This knowledge of causal relationships and parameters is the basis on which the new technology is constructed. In the present case the sequence of events has been reversed. We seem to have a technology that works but we do not really know why.[9]

Although the educational benefits of simulation games have not been rigorously measured there are numerous testimonials asserting that participation in simulation games has significant educational benefits.[10] Experience in simulation games has led to

---

[7]Chadwick F. Alger: *Simulation in International Relations.* R. C. Snyder, Ed., p. 151.
[8]Sarane S. Boocock and E. O. Schild: *Simulation Games in Learning.* p. 17.
[9]*Ibid.*, p. 22.
[10]Alger: *loc. cit.*

several conclusions regarding these benefits. Simulation games heighten the interest and motivation of the player through experience with an enjoyable activity, extensive involvement and continued activity outside the class through sharing a common experience with others. It also provides a laboratory in which a player can apply a wide variety of concepts, tools, and strategies learned from books, teachers, outside sources, and prior experiences. In most simulation games the player is part of a group involved in decision-making. He experiences the ways in which decisions are shaped by group relationships and the way roles are defined within the group.

Experience is gained in actually making decisions rather than simply evaluating the decisions of others through the case study method. Simulation game experience also offers insights into decision-making processes that are peculiar to the system under study.[11]

THE BASIC FORMS

In this day and age simulation seems to be all around us. We hear a great deal about simulation in our day-to-day contacts. Simulators have been designed to allow astronauts to experience, in a laboratory setting, the tasks and activities associated with space travel.[12] The Southern Pacific Railroad is presently operating a locomotive simulator at the McDonnell Douglas Corporation facility at Downey, California. This one million dollar system built by the McDonnell Douglas Corporation can simulate the operation of a diesel locomotive and the operation of a train up to two-hundred cars in length. It consists of a full size mock-up of a diesel locomotive cab, a wide angle color movie screen and is capable of simulating all of the oral, visual, and motion cues associated with the operation of said locomotive and/or train. With the aid of a computer the simulator is able to present to the operator problem situations found in the operation of a diesel locomotive. The simulator is also able to physically respond

---

[11]*Ibid.*, pp. 152-153.
[12]Harney: *op. cit.*, p. 1.

to the operation of the controls of the simulated locomotive through the form of oral, visual, and motion cues. Through the computer the instructor is able to vary the operating conditions and record the operator's responses for later evaluation.[13]

In Denver, Colorado, United Airlines maintains a thirty million dollar training facility where they have eighteen jet simulators valued at twelve million dollars. The training center was originally built by the city of Denver after a twenty-five million dollar bond issue was passed by the voters. The facility has a permanent teaching staff of 650 instructors who conduct a ground school, which incorporates the use of flight simulators in the training program. United trains 800 new pilots annually and over 5000 airline pilots return to the facility for recurrent training twice a year. The jet simulators look like the front end of a regular jetliner with the nose beveled off. It sits on what resembles a giant tuning fork. As a flight progresses it moves up and down or inclines in the direction of a turn. The windows are blacked over and the physical characteristics of airports are projected on a television screen in front of the simulator as the crew maneuvers it. The interior of the simulator is a full size mock-up of the cockpit in the jetliner simulated. At the back of the cockpit is a console with over one hundred buttons. Each of these buttons, if pushed, present one of several emergency situations to the operator through oral, visual and/or motion cues. With the aid of a computer the instructor can trigger emergencies that never happen in years of line flying so that if something does go wrong the instructor can instruct the operator as to the proper procedure. The simulator adds a realism to training which allows flight crews to obtain a high degree of proficiency before they ever step into an airplane.

Simulations have been designed to provide television viewers information and visual insight into space missions such as the Apollo flights.[14] They are also used in education and training programs.

---

[13]First Films for Simulator Completed, *Southern Pacific Bulletin*, (August-September, 1969), p. 6.

[14]Harney: *loc. cit.*

Symbolic simulation is used extensively in the business and operations research fields. This type of simulation can best be typified by the business computer game where all aspects are reduced to symbols. These symbols are then played against a previously programmed computer which provides feedback to the player regarding the results of his actions.[15] The business decision-maker is thus provided with experience in many fields such as marketing, product design possibilities, budgeting, etc.

Operational simulation is a form of simulation which usually deals with operational systems.[16] The basic applications of this type are as follows: the testing of the adequacy of operational systems, training members of operational staffs, and as an educational device at most levels in the educational system. This form of simulation usually consists of a role-playing-crisis playing game where each player of the group assumes a role and is confronted individually or as a group with one or more problems requiring a decision. Some of the advantages of this form of simulation are that it tends to develop problem solving attitudes, forces individuals to work together, defines areas of individual responsibility, identifies the need for additional planning, identifies information needs and identifies additional training needs.[17]

There are four basic component elements in operational simulation: design objectives, the model, the scenario, and the necessary replications.[18]

The design objectives will depend largely upon the needs of the exercise designer. This is one of the most important elements and it is especially important that the objectives be well specified and that they do not compete with one another. A few examples of design objectives are to test emergency procedures, to determine the maximum system load, to determine decision information needs, to train members of an operational staff, improve decision-making techniques, to determine resource requirements and/or test operational equipment.

---

[15]Harney: *op. cit.*, pp. 1-2.
[16]Richard A. Brody: *Simulation in International Relations*. Richard C. Snyder, Ed., pp. 200-202.
[17]Harney: *op. cit.*, p. 9.
[18]Harney: *op. cit.*, p. 3.

The operational model will deal with the players, their interface points, and the procedures of that system. It is important to know with whom you will be dealing, the extent of contact with the external environment, and the procedures for dealing with the external environment.

The scenario or problem setting is a chronological description of the significant events that are to take place during the simulation exercise. The scenario must follow directly from the specified objectives and will contain problems, information, and events.

The replications are the physical facilities, the required communications, and the job aids in general which are required to conduct the simulation exercise. Research simulation exercises held in laboratory settings are very effective but to obtain the maximum training benefits it is preferred that the facility resemble reality. They should simulate the player's own environment, resources, and problems so that the player will act more naturally to the inputs.[19]

An example of operational simulation is an exercise held by the Air Pollution Control Institute, School of Public Administration, University of Southern California. The exercise is called "Mapcore" and simulates a County Health Department in operation. The group theoretically is the entity handling air pollution problems within the county. The players assume the roles of the director of health and his staff. During the exercise the full array of problems which they might face are thrown at them including calls from irate citizens, the county commission, and the press. While playing out their roles the players are furnished additional routine problems through written communications presented to them through their respective in-baskets. The entire session is video taped.

At the end of the exercise the tape is played back during a critique session where the players are given an overview of the exercise and they are able to critique their respective decisions.[20]

---

[19]Harney: *op. cit.*, pp. 2-4.

[20]Information concerning "Mapcore" was obtained through a personal interview with Dr. R. Brandford Jones, Training Coordinator, Civil Defense Training Program, University of Southern California.

Another example of operational simulation is a complex exercise in emergency operations. This exercise is also conducted by Dr. Jones under the Civil Defense Training Program, School of Public Administration, University of Southern California. Emergency Operations Simulation Training has been developed through the Department of Defense, Office of Civil Defense, so that local communities could have training in the concept of emergency operations. The standard operating configuration is shown in the following illustration. The Operations Room is supported by a number of communications systems which link it with simulated operating services of the community, simulated National Warning System, simulated Emergency Broadcast System, simulated local military and civilian organizations and simulated adjacent and higher governmental agencies. These systems are assumed to be fully operational.

Incoming communications are received and recorded on the proper form by a communications staff member. They are then forwarded by appropriate messenger to the Operations Room. The flow of information in the form of messages to and from the communications center is provided for by a controller and a staff of messengers. In addition players in the Operations Room may make direct communications with the simulated outside agencies and vice versa. The Operations Room staff also includes a number of plotters who update and maintain control displays according to determined procedures. These displays provide timely information of various types to the players. On the basis of the written inputs and other information supplied through the various displays and other communication systems, the players make the necessary decisions and allocate the proper resources to cope with the emergency at hand. Those actions that involve the commitment of resources are reduced to writing on the proper forms. These actions are then recorded on the appropriate Operations Room displays, forwarded to the communication center and then dispatched to the addressee.[21]

---

[21]*Emergency Operations Simulation Training Operations Manual*, SM-4.1.1, January 1967, pp. 1, 3, 5.

Police Disaster Operations

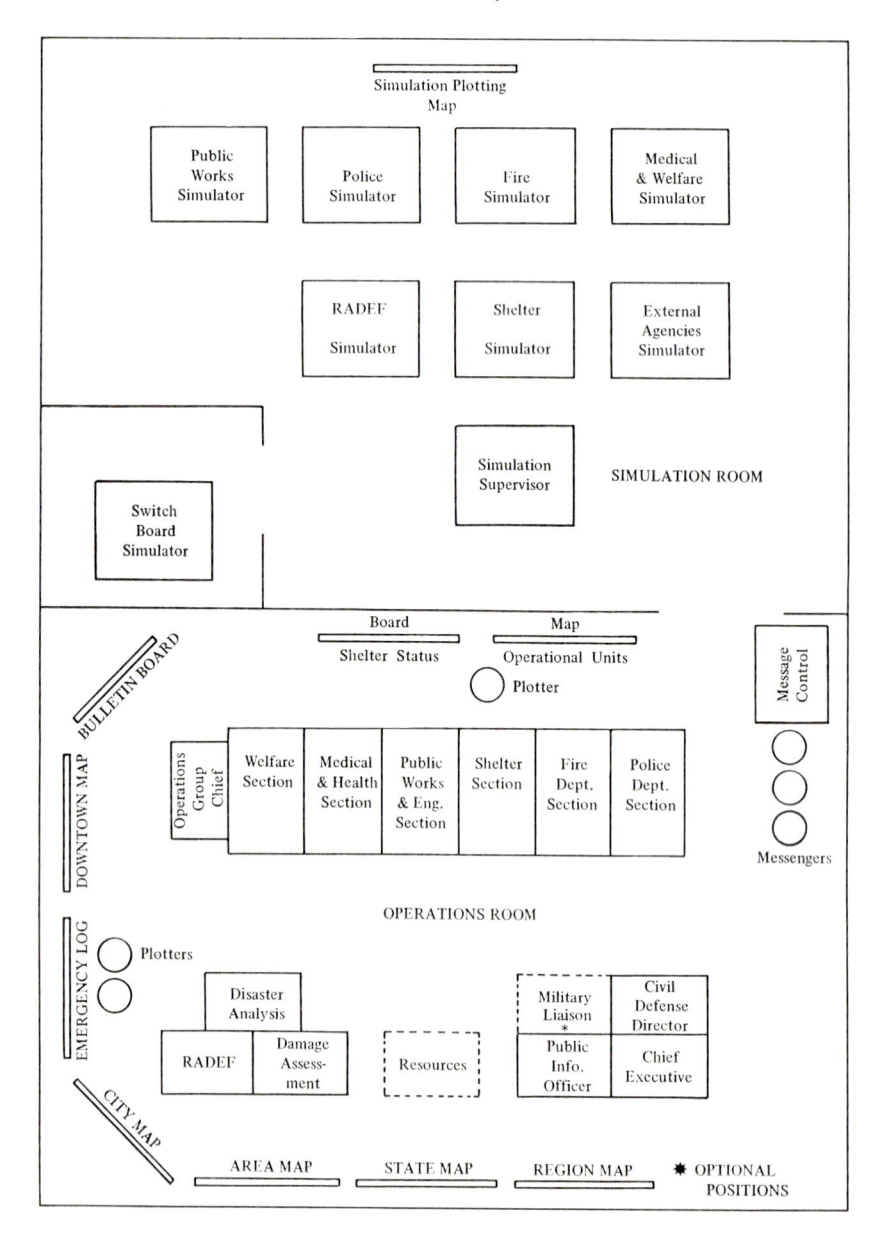

SIMULATION ROOM

- Simulation Plotting Map
- Public Works Simulator
- Police Simulator
- Fire Simulator
- Medical & Welfare Simulator
- RADEF Simulator
- Shelter Simulator
- External Agencies Simulator
- Simulation Supervisor
- Switch Board Simulator

OPERATIONS ROOM

- Board: Shelter Status
- Map: Operational Units — Plotter
- Bulletin Board
- Downtown Map
- Emergency Log
- City Map
- Message Control
- Messengers

Sections: Operations Group Chief | Welfare Section | Medical & Health Section | Public Works & Eng. Section | Shelter Section | Fire Dept. Section | Police Dept. Section

Plotters

- Disaster Analysis
- RADEF
- Damage Assessment
- Resources
- Military Liaison *
- Civil Defense Director
- Public Info. Officer
- Chief Executive

Area Map — State Map — Region Map

✱ OPTIONAL POSITIONS

In the exercise the Simulation Room represents the external environment to the Operations Room. It generally consists of nine simulation positions.
1. Simulation Supervisor.
2. Police Simulator.
3. Fire Simulator.
4. Public Works and Engineering Simulator.
5. Medical and Welfare Simulator.
6. Shelter Simulator.
7. RADEF Simulator.
8. External Agencies Simulator.
9. Switchboard Operator Simulator.

It is the responsibility of the Simulation Supervisor to oversee and coordinate all activities within the Simulation Room. Adequate simulation requires a thoroughly trained staff of simulators who are familiar with their respective roles and responsibilities, are knowledgeable in the operational area being simulated, cognizant of the general sequence of major events programmed for the exercise and thoroughly familiar with the prescribed situations prepared for their respective areas. The simulator must first and foremost know who he is supposed to be. Whether he is preparing a written message or talking to operational personnel on the telephone, he must be prepared to simulate one of many people. Each simulator is assigned an area of responsibility for providing simulation. This simulation takes two forms, verbal and written. Written information is forwarded to the Operations Room on one of the message forms, through the Simulation Supervisor who is responsible for checking the messages for completeness and coherence. Verbal information is given directly over the telephone to the Operations Room staff.

Written inputs are of two types. The first type is in the form of prescribed messages prepared for the exercise prior to its actual operation. These represent programmed situations built into the exercise. The second type are called dynamic inputs and are in response to messages coming out of the Operations Room or are spontaneous in nature resulting from the general operation of the exercise. In order to control the flow of communications from the Simulation Room to the Operations Room all messages are directed through the Simulation Supervisor. The messages are filed in a time ordered pile on his desk. Messengers then pick up the messages at the proper time and distribute them to the Operations Room staff. Feedback is usually directed to the Operations Room through the Simulation Room in the form of new problems resulting from the decisions made by members of the Operations Room staff.[22] All operations in the Operations Room are recorded for future use during a critique session at the end of the exercise.

III. ELEMENTARY SIMULATION DESIGN

As mentioned before the most important item in simulation design is to have well specified objectives which do not compete with each other. There are many possible objectives which should be considered. A few of the more important are as follows: test procedures, test the system, train the staff, determine the maximum load of the system, determine decision-making information needs, research in complex systems, determine resource needs, determine the capacity of operational staff members under load and identify future training needs. The total number of objectives will depend on the needs of the exercise designer.

After the objectives have been identified and defined, they are then specified in terms of substantive scope, structural comprehension, factual detail and relationships to other material. These objectives are then used to limit the situation or process to be analyzed in time, geographic area, functional scope, and detail. This time, area, function, and space problem is then subjected to a system analysis. This analysis consists of identifying all of the major decision-making entities, their material information inputs, outputs, their resources, and the information exchanged by the decision-making elements.

---

[22]*Emergency Operations Simulation Training, Simulation Manual,* SM-4.1.2, January 1967, pp. 1, 3-6.

A sequential analysis is then made to determine the sequence and rate of flow of information and resources among the respective decision-making entities previously identified. This analysis determines the information and resource inputs of each entity.

A decision analysis is then made on the entities in question. This process is to determine what operations the entities perform on their respective information and resource inputs in order to produce their decisions or outputs. It is much easier to identify the alternative decision rules or criterion for a particular entity after their respective inputs and outputs have been specified over a range of typical conditions. A decision-making analysis usually identifies the relative stable criterion or motives for decision-making entities by dividing them into absolute and instrumental values.

A decision analysis determines which problems are perceived in which way. Problems may be defined as discrepancies between the ideal state perceived by the particular entity and the perceived actual state. The problem is followed by a problem solving response which may range from denial that the problem exists to the decision to allocate and engage various resources to correct the discrepancies, under consideration. The criterion for the allocation and engagement of resources to correct the problem usually include the expectations of relative cost, risk and effectiveness of alternative responses. In short the system analysis identifies the actors, their interactions and their decision-making rules in response to the problems presented.

Given the model of decision-making entities obtained through system analysis it remains to translate this analytical model into a human player simulation game which will communicate the results and implications of the analysis to the player. To communicate effectively the model must be translated into a game that will capture the interest of and motivate the player. It also must enable the player to experiment actively with the consequences of various moves or changes in the system under study. The particular simulation game will depend largely upon the time, space, cost, number, and capacity of the players.

The game teams, player objectives, allowable activities, rules, and win-lose criterion are then developed in light of the previously outlined objectives. The game design involves the establishment of a fine line between realism and playability. The closer the game comes to reality the more cumbersome it becomes until it is no longer playable. The simulation game design should be refined prior to placing it into final operation. This is accomplished through a series of exercises in which problems of clumsiness and distortion are identified and eliminated. In tuning up the game certain trade-offs must be considered against the objectives. The most common are between realism and playability, between concentration and comprehensiveness and between melodramatic motivation and analytical calm. Each element must be given a relative weight which must be considered against the overall objectives.[23]

Time should be allocated for a critique session after the completion of the exercise. This aspect of the exercise should prove very fruitful and stimulating. The critique should consist of a review of the exercise by the instructor or operator. The operator or instructor should also include his observations regarding the outputs of the players during the exercise. Each player should be given the opportunity to critique his performance noting any changes he would make regarding his performance and what he has learned from the total experience.[24]

REFERENCES

Books

Anonymous: *Top Management Decision Simulation.* New York, American Medical Association, 1957.

Anderson, Lee F.: *A Comparison of Simulation, Case Studies and Problem Papers in Decision Making.* Evanston, Ill., Northwestern University Press, 1964.

Boocock, Sarane S. and Schild, E. O.: *Simulation Games in Learning.* Beverly Hills, Sage Publishing Inc., 1968.

---

[23]Boocock and Schild: *op. cit.,* pp. 75-77.
[24]Andlinger: *loc. cit.*

Bosil, Douglas C.: *Executive Decision-Making Through Simulation.* Columbus, Ohio, Merrill Books, 1965.
Greene, J. R. and Sisson, R. L.: *Dynamic Management Decision Games.* New York, Wiley and Sons, 1959.
Guetzkow, Harold S.: *Simulation in Social Science.* Englewood Cliffs, N.J., Prentice Hall, 1962.
Snyder, Richard C.: *Simulation in International Relations.* Englewood Cliffs, N.J., Prentice Hall, 1963.
Tocher, K.: *The Art of Simulation.* Princeton, N.J., Van Nostrand, 1963.

Bibliographies

Hellebrandt, E. T. and Fleishhacker, W. D.: *General Business Management Simulation* (Processed). Athens, Ohio University, 1959.
Riley, V. and Young, J. P.: *Bibliography on War Games* (Processed). Chevy Chase, The Johns Hopkins University, 1959.
Shubik, Martin: Bibliography on simulation gaming, artificial intelligence and allied topics, *The American Statistical Association Journal,* LV:736-751. December, 1960.

Papers and Articles

Anonymous: Operational games in industry, *Operations Research for Management, II,* J. McClouskey and J. M. Coppinger (Eds.) Baltimore, The Johns Hopkins Press, 1956.
_____. War games and operations research, *Philosophy of Science.* 22:4, October, 1955.
_____: Top Management Decision-Making Simulation, *Report of System Simulation Symposium.* D. G. Malcolm (Ed.) Baltimore, Waverly Press, 1957.
_____: War games for the business man, *The Economist.* June 29, 1957.
_____:Techniques of system analysis, *The Rand Corporation.* RM 1829, December 3, 1956.
_____: *Simulation Its Uses and Potential, Part II,* (Processed) New York, General Electric Company, Expository and Development Paper No. 3, May 4, 1959.
_____: Industrial dynamics a major breakthrough for decision-making, *The Harvard Business Review,* 36:4, July-August, 1958.
_____: First films for simulator completed, *Southern Pacific Bulletin,* August-September, 1969.
Andlinger, G. R.: Business games—Play one, *Harvard Business Review,* 36:2, March-April, 1958.

Blake, R. R. and Brehm, J. W.: The use of tape recordings to simulate a group atmosphere, *Small Groups: Studies in Social Interaction.* A. P. Hare, et al. (Eds.), New York, Alfred Knopf, 1955.

Brooks, F. C. and Hill, F. I. A laboratory for combat operations research, *Or Jorsa*, 5:6, December, 1957.

Chapman, Charles C.: Training to meet unusual occurrences, *Police*, May-June, 1962.

Christie, L. S.: Organization and Information Handling in Task Groups, *Or Jorsa*, December 2, 1954.

Clark, C. E., Malcolm, D. G., Craft, C. J., and Ricciardi, F. M.: On the construction of a multi-stage, multi-person business game, *Or Jorsa*, 5:4, August, 1957.

Cushen, W. E.: Generalized Battle Games on a Digital Computer, *Operations Research Technical Memorandum*, Operations Research Office, T-263.

Cyert, R. M., Dearborn, D. C., Dill, W. R., et al.: The C.I.T. Management Game, *Pittsburg: The Carnegie Institute of Technology*, April, 1958.

Deemer, W. L., Jr.: The role of operational gaming in operations research, *Or Jorsa*, 5:1, February, 1957.

Harling, J.: Simulation techniques in operational research, *Operational Research Quarterly*, 9:1, March, 1958. Reprinted in *Or Jorsa*, 6:3, May-June, 1958.

Harney, Terence P. Simulation applications for disaster command and control, *Systems Development Corporation*, SP-3368, July 15, 1969, Santa Monica, California.

Maxwell, W. L.: Some problems of digital systems simulation, *Management Science*, 6:1, October, 1959.

McDonald, J.: The business decision game, *Fortune*, March, 1958.

Ricciardi, F. M.: Business war games for executives: A new concept in management training, *Management Review*, 46:5, May, 1957.

Shubik, M.: Business gaming (Processed), *New York: General Electric Company, Expository and Development Paper No. 5*, June 9, 1958.

F
MODEL DISASTER RESPONSE PLAN

INFORMATION ATTACHMENT

1. Security position—selected for their protection from blast damage—one in each patrol district. See special order on *Police Survival Under Nuclear Attack*.
2. Reconnaissance positions (two in each patrol district)—see map—selected for the following:
   a. access to main road net.
   b. radio communications advantage.
   c. telepone accessibility.
3. Code 20—see *Special Order on Press Relations*.
4. Prisoner evacuation—see *Jail Order*.
5. Switchboard control—see order on *Emergency Communications*, and instructions for use of unlisted telephone.
6. Call-up system—All personnel have complete up-to-date list of departmental personnel by name, address, and at least three phone numbers for each.
   a. Desk officer will telephone until he reaches two officers—he will assign one to call all others A to M and the other to call all officers N to Z.
   b. If telephones are out of service contact will be made personally.
   c. Note: Radio and television stations may broadcast signal _____. Report to the station at once when this signal is used.

Police Disaster Operations

ALERT (code _____)
(Notice of any pending Disaster or Disturbance)

COMMUNICATIONS RECORDS INVESTIGATION (1-4 men)	PATROL (5-9 men)	COMMAND (1-2 men)
CLOSE SWITCHBOARD USE UNLISTED PHONE Set up for *man-power* *call-up* Routine Notification of other agencies Freeze off-duty officers Ready Prisoners for evacuation or release Ready special equipment as indicated Set up emergency battery operated radio Patrol Car or Handy-Talki OPEN SWITCHBOARD WHEN POSSIBLE	Disengage Activity Move to Reconnaissance Position–Code 2	EVALUATE in Field or at Station ORDER: 1. Return to normal 2. Disturbance plan 3. Disaster plan 4. Nuclear plan

ACTION-DISTURBANCE

Close Switchboard
 	
Call-up system off-duty and reserve officers.
 	
Cordon and Assistance request.
  1. Other Police Agencies
  2. Other Agencies
 	
Code 20 for press, radio and T.V.
 	
Surplus Personnel to Assembly Point; Special equipment
  1. Gas
  2. Camera
 	
Convert Ambulance to Prisoner Transportation Wagon
 	
OPEN SWITCHBOARD WHEN POSSIBLE
	Designated unit to handle other major crime incidents during emergency.
	Other Units to Assembly Point
	  1. No unit to respond to location of disturbance.
	  2. Code 2 response only
		Designate:
		  1. Assembly point
		  2. Cordon points
		  3. Units to respond
		
		Declare:
		  1. Disaster area
		  2. Unlawful Assem.
		
		Command:
		  1. At scene

ACTION -- DISASTER

COMMUNICATIONS RECORDS INVESTIGATION (1-4 men)	PATROL (5-9 men)	COMMAND (1-2 men)
Close Switchboard	Designated Unit to handle major crime incidents during emergency	Conduct Reconnaissance
Call-up system off-duty and reserve officers		Assign personnel as needed with emphasis on:
Activate Mutual-Aid	Other Units to Station or Assembly Point as designated	1. Evacuation. 2. Cordon off area to protect public. 3. Protection of life and property.
Code 20 for press, radio and T.V.		
Notify special C.D. personnel		Declare Disaster Area
OPEN SWITCHBOARD WHEN POSSIBLE		Secondary Emphasis 1. Recover injured 2. Recover and Identify dead.

ACTION -- NUCLEAR ATTACK

Close Switchboard	Move from Recon. position to Security Position	Insure maximum dispersal of man-power and equipment.
Blanket Parole Prisoners -- Release		
Ready Station as per C.D. instructions	Take precautions for security	Go to DISASTER PLAN after blast.
Personnel to basement.	Respond after blast as ordered.	Implement special C.D. functions.
Battery operated radio set up in basement.		1. Radioactive Monitoring. 2. Explosive recon.
Special Files to Basement.		
Respond after blast as per disaster plan.		

G
DISASTER RESPONSE SIMULATIONS

Simulation exercises for police disaster response may be created for agencies of almost any size. Realism is essential: time span, communications, and roles must be identical to actual situations. The basis for the exercise is the script, which controls the content and direction of the simulation.

Since the primary input of stimulation for police action is the telephone, the script is reduced to a tape containing telephone messages at an appropriate interval. During the first portion of the simulation these calls require routine police action; later the calls will relate both to the disaster and routine matters.

Disaster response simulation replicates small police department station staff: watch commander, records clerk, desk officer and dispatcher.

As patrol cars are dispatched and respond, their radio messages constitute a second type of stimulation for decisions made by the watch commander. These communications are controlled by referees or cue cards.

Each simulation must have definite objectives with respect to training or testing: evacuation, mutual aid, or manpower recall. It is wise to include only a few objectives in each simulation and to establish them before writing the script. The script must be kept secret from those participating.

The simulations described here were developed for a small department and are based on the following manpower:

Watch Commander—Lieutenant	1
Patrol Sergeant	1
Desk Officer	1
Dispatcher	1
Detective	1
Patrol Car Officers	5

Instructions for the officers involved in the simulation are as follows:

WATCH COMMANDER

The watch commander in this simulated exercise plays the key role in that he determines the response to the stimuli presented in the program. In order to intelligently respond, he must have some idea of what manpower, facilities, and equipment is available to him and he must also have some knowledge of the physical workings of the simulator. The first half of this requirement is easily met as the response will necessarily be limited to within the scope of each individual department.

The second prerequisite for an intelligent response, a knowledge of the physical workings of this simulator, is presented here.

We will create a police station, the personnel to man the station, and a disaster. The watch commander, responding to the stimulus, will react to the disaster as he sees fit. He will have an appropriate combination of the following personnel.

1. *A desk officer.* His duties will normally be to answer the phone. This officer shall be considered sworn personnel and he will carry out his duties as directed by the watch commander.
2. *A dispatcher.* His duties would normally be to assist in answering phones, to maintain a unit log, and to dispatch radio cars. He is sworn personnel and will carry out his duties as directed by the watch commander.
3. *A sergeant.* His duty is supervision of the desk function and of field operations. He will carry out his duties as directed by the watch commander.
4. *A detective.* His duties would be to conduct immediate follow-up investigation in the case of a serious crime. While not assigned to the patrol division, it is assumed he would carry out any orders issued by the watch commander.
5. As many radio cars as would normally be fielded by your individual department. Each unit will be manned by a capable officer with all the equipment he would normally have.

In addition to the manpower as shown above, the watch commander will have at his disposal all the equipment his department would normally have on hand, or be able to procure for use during the disaster. Further if his department has any emergency mobilization plan or any mutual aid pacts, the watch commander is encouraged to utilize them if he feels circumstances warrant it.

The watch commander's response must be limited to the scope within which his department would be able to respond. His orders will be carried out as they would under any other situation. He may utilize his manpower and equipment any way he sees fit.

There will be radio communication with all units. Should the desk sergeant be sent to the scene of the disaster, or should the watch commander respond, it will be assumed that he goes in a radio car and he too will have radio communication. The length of time it takes for him to arrive will be determined by a referee.

By the same token should any mutual aid pacts be implemented, or should a department mobilization be called, the number of radio cars sent or the length of time it takes for men to arrive at the station will also be determined by the referee.

Although the watch commander will be physically separated from the units in the field, referees will be available to serve as liaison. Referees will be prepared to answer any question that does not affect the handling of the situation.

The basic purpose of the simulation is to train ranking officers to be better prepared to cope with disasters, riots, and other major police problems that are unanticipated. The person playing the role of watch commander is encouraged to use any and all facilities he has available. The determination as to whether or not each item is realistic will be made by a referee. All activities will be recorded, either on tape or on paper by the referees, with all participants being able to engage in a critique at the conclusion of the problem.

Post simulation critique is most important to discover deficiencies in plans or equipment and to determine new training needs.

DESK OFFICER

Function: Basic purpose is to answer all incoming calls and decide their classification.

Duties: Maintain a log or call slips; time received; disposition.

You are subject to the desk sergeant (and/or the watch commander). You should attempt to answer all calls unless directed to do otherwise.

All assigned calls given to the dispatcher should be placed on a "dispatch form" first and that form given to him.

Use proper police and Penal Code classifications, when possible, or as appropriate to your department.

Limitations: You are not to make decisions, unless directed to do so by a higher authority.

When handed a "key" card by a referee, you must follow instructions regarding information received. How it is used or evaluated is up to the desk sergeant or the watch commander.

Telephone communication (taped calls) are to be received until directed otherwise by a higher authority (regular days business).

Summary: Information received by you should be passed on to the dispatcher and/or the desk sergeant for action.

DISPATCHER

Function: To dispatch calls to the field units and receive information from them.

Duties: You receive calls to dispatch from the desk officer.

Generally you have the prerogative to dispatch available units as you so desire.

Maintain a log or call slips to show the following:
1. Type of call dispatched.
2. Unit that received it.
3. Time detailed to the unit.
4. Time unit arrived at the scene.
5. Disposition.

Information received from the field regarding activity should be placed on the "dispatch form."

Any major decision should be checked with the desk sergeant unless otherwise directed by him.

Attempt when possible to use Penal Code and "10" code designations.

Always answer the field unit requests whenever possible.

You will receive "key" cards from your referee. You must follow the directions in reference to dispatches he requires you to make. Subsequent action is up to you and the people in the problem.

It is suggested you confer with the desk sergeant whenever possible.

Summary: You are the main artery for the field units and they will be very dependent upon you. Your radio designation when speaking as the station will be the word "control."

The gray communication set up before you ideally would be a three-way system. The field units will be able to hear each call that you dispatch to them and the replies of the other field units.

PATROL OFFICERS

There are several radio stations hooked into a master voice control (base station). Each unit is a simulated radio car—from time to time during the exercise one or more persons may be designated by the referee to act in another capacity, such as a field sergeant, detective unit, or field commander.

There are several sets of cue cards. Incidents will be dispatched from the base station. The person operating the predesignated numbered patrol car will acknowledge the call and follow the instructions on the cue card.

As this exercise progresses, the referee will assign other problem cards to various cars to report to the base station.

SCRIPT ONE

This simulation is developed around an airplane crash and tests the watch commander in several techniques:
1. Manpower recall.
2. Mutual aid requests.
3. Command post establishment.
4. Maintaining police service in the community.
5. Conducting an evacuation.

This simulation was developed for a department that does not share its radio frequency with neighboring agencies.

Police Disaster Operations

Min. into Tape	Note -- Tape starts at 1900 hours. Recorded message to desk officer.	Probable Desk Action	Patrol Car Messages
1901	This is Mrs. Parks of 907 Alameda Ave. The kids were playing in the vacant lot out back and they found an old safe. It's empty now, but there is a big hole in the bottom -- and it looks suspicious.	Probable dispatch #1	Acknowledge call (this becomes unit #1 in script)
1902	When can I bring my kid and his new bike down for bike tags? The kid has a small motor on it now, and I wonder, do you still give it a bike tag, or does he have to get a motorcycle tag from the State?		
1904	This is Tom Grimes at the Standard Station at Verdugo and Olive. A truck just came down the hill without brakes and hit another truck about one half block south on Olive. I think one guy is hurt cause they have him out on the street and he is just lying there.	Probable dispatch #2	Acknowledge call (this unit becomes #2 in script)
1904½	This is Tim O'Connor of 1601 Olive. There's been a hell of an accident here. A truck is all over my yard and ruined one of my trees. I want some pictures taken because somebody has to pay for my tree.		Unit #1 goes out of service on call and stays off the air.
1905½	This is Mrs. Jones of 4520 Verdugo. There has been a terrible explosion up the street. I can see flames 100 feet high. It looks like about Verdugo and Cordova. Everyone is running up toward there, but I thought I should call you.	Probable dispatch #3	Unit #2 goes out of service on call Unit sent to explosion acknowledges (becomes #3 in script)
1906	This is Lloyd Smythe of 201 Cordova. An airplane just came over and crashed up the street. I think it sounded like a jet. There was a big explosion. It just missed my house. It even took off my TV antenna.		Unit #2 requests ambulance and tow truck, has 2 injuries.
1907	This is the fire dispatcher, we have a report on a major fire at Verdugo and Cordova -- Fire units are Code 3. Possible airplane crash.	Dispatch from this point is not predictable.	Unit #3 reports major fire at Verdugo & Cordova.
1907½	This is Myrtle Thompson of the Board of Education. I am going to try to get a new credential and I need to be fingerprinted. When should I come down.		
1908	This is Leroy Larson of 401 Rose Street. I'm calling from the corner payphone. My wife has locked me out and I want to go back for my stuff -- but I want a cop to standby so there isn't any trouble. She says she will kill me if I come back -- but I don't even have my shoes.		Unit #3 reports many burn victims in street -- request ambulance.
1909	Can you settle an argument for my dad and me. I say that you can smoke when you are 18 and he says you can't 'til you're 21 -- the same as drinking?		Unit #1 advises recovered safe, requests detective.
1910	I want to know if you give out parking tickets in the downtown area, between 2 and 5 in the morning. We are going to do an inventory tonight and I want to leave my car out in front of the street where I can watch it.		Messages from this point become controlled by referee, except as indicated.

Disaster Response Simulations

1911	This is Fenton Archibald of 601 Lima Street. It's about the airplane crash. I went over but I can't find an officer to report to — and the firemen won't even listen to me. There's a body in my garage. It came right through the roof. It's still strapped in a seat. What should I do?		
1911½	This is Speedy Type of the Clarion Daily News. What do you guys have there. We haven't got a Code 20 yet.		
1912	Can you give me the number of the City Pound or Humane Society. Our cat has died. The garage door came down on her.		
1913	This is Mrs. Clover at 307 Beechwood. Can you send a car right away. Someone is breaking into our garage.		
1914	This is the fire dispatcher. Chief Thompson has just requested mutual aid from all surrounding fire departments. There will be an undetermined number of fire trucks Code 3 within the city limits.		
1914½	This is the supervising operator. Several main telephone trunks are out of order in the Verdugo park area due to a fire. The overload may affect your telephone service. Please use your prefix 271 telephones for outgoing calls.		Any unit at the disaster scene requests help for crowd control.
1915	This is Lt. Grover of North Pasadena Police Department — We have had no telephone service until now, but we have been monitoring daleglen radio. Do you need mutual aid? We can give you 5 men and 2 cars.		
1915½	This is the fire dispatcher. Chief Thompson requests police crowd and traffic control for a perimeter of Clark on the north, Olive on the south, Pass Ave. on the west, and California on the east. He is unable to contact any police units at the location.		
1916	This is LeRoy McCall calling from Daleglen. Do you have my brother Paul in jail? We were getting phone calls from him every few minutes until about 15 minutes ago and he was pretty drunk. He lives at 403 Avon. We are very worried, could you have an officer check the house for us?		
1917	This is Cuff of K.R.A.P. Can you tell us the best route to follow to get to the airplane crash. We will have a TV camera truck.		Any unit at scene advises that two Sheriffs units arrived at his location and request assignment.
1917½	Can you give me Officer Johnson's telephone number at home? I have to call him about a very important matter.		
1918	This is Doctor Grunder of the Valley Clinic. Do you need me at the scene of the airplane crash?		Any unit at scene advises fire department request evacuation of population — requests advise.
1918½	This is the fire dispatcher. Chief Thompson advises that the fire is endangering the propane tanks at Columbia Ranch. He requests immediate evacuation of all persons within the perimeter of Clark, Olive, Pass, and California.		
1919	We would like to book the police band for our school. Who should we talk to?		
1919½	This is Elmo Furgeson of 461 Onterio. Some gal just wandered into our yard and she is out of her mind. She keeps yelling that they are all burned up. We can't find out her name and she is scaring hell out of the kids. You better come get her.		

SCRIPT TWO

This simulation is developed around an earthquake and tidal wave. It tests the ability of the watch commander to accomplish the following:

1. Decide on granting mutual aid.
2. Establish a manpower recall.
3. Conduct an evacuation.

It was developed for a coastal department which shares its radio frequency with neighboring agencies, and to make the exercise realistic a second recorder was used with a tape which simulated the sheriffs radio communications.

Min. into Tape	Recorded Message to Desk Officer	Probable Desk Action	Message Over Sheriff's Radio	Patrol Car Messages
1901	Mr. James R. Stevenson, 473 Abbott Street reports his window has just been broken by juveniles in the area.	Probable dispatch # 1	Routine Sheriffs calls and responses related to their jurisdictions.	Acknowledge call (this becomes unit # 1 in script.)
1901	Mr. Stone at the Sears Store in the Esplanda Shopping Center reports that a customer is creating a disturbance in his store.	Probable dispatch # 2		Acknowledge call (This becomes unit # 2 in script.)
1902½	Mrs. Janet Roberts wants to know when the police auction is going to take place and where.			
1903	Mr. Robert Brown, 463 Ashton St., wants information on a traffic ticket that he got for changing lanes without a signal and interfering with another vehicle.			Unit # 1 goes out of service at location.
1905	Mr. Carmack, Bank of A. Levy, Fifth and A Streets reports an abandoned vehicle left on his parking lot.	Possible dispatch # 3		Acknowledge call (this becomes unit # 3 in script.)
1906	Mr. Jose Navarro, 574 Ferrara Way, wants to talk to detectives regarding a check case he is involved in.			
1906½	Rev. Dan Genung 321 Maple St., wants a speaker to talk to a youth group on narcotics for this Sunday at his church.			Unit # 2 goes out of service at call.
1907	EARTHQUAKE OCCURRED HERE -- NO OUTSIDE NOTIFICATION IS NECESSARY (CARD TO LT.)			Card to units.
1907½	Mrs. Emma Croller 516 LaCanada, wants to know what has just happened, was it some kind of explosion?	Dispatch from this point is not predictable.	Dispatcher advises that Sheriffs Facility is in good order and they are broadcasting on auxiliary generator.	
1908	Mrs. Lucy Johnson 519 Gloria Ct., "my roof has fallen in and there is a child trapped in the room."			Unit # 3 at location of call -- reports earthquake.
1909	Mr. Robert Solas, "I am at the corner of Wooley Rd., & Oxnard St., the gasoline drums under ground here at the Texaco Service Station have exploded and that his building is on fire as well as the building next to him".			Unit #2 reports he has misd. suspect in custody -- shall he transport or release to clear for emergency call.
1909¼	Bill Thompson, city electrician calls to determine if emergency generator is OK.		Routine Sheriffs dispatches re: earthquake.	Unit # 1 reports back in service, Juvs. G.P.A. -- misc. damage report.
1909½	Mr. Ralph Householder at the Enco Station Wooley Rd., and Oxnard reports that there are hot lines down and blocking Oxnard Rd.and the street has buckled and is passable if the lines can be removed..." HEY AN EXPLOSION HAS SET THE TEXACO SERVICE STATION ON FIRE AND THE BUILDINGS AROUND IT!"			Patrol unit messages directed by referee from this point.

Disaster Response Simulations

1910	Anonymous, at Saviors Rd. and Highway 1 there are lots of buildings on fire and the service stations on all the corners are on fire.		
1910½	Mr. R. Davis, reports that at 3rd and Oxnard Rd. hot lines are in the street and numerous telephone and electric poles are blocking Oxnard Road.		
1911	Bookkeeper, Furniture Store Corner Eighth St. and Oxnard, broken windows and injury — wants ambulance.		
1912	Public Service reports that all electricity has failed and numerous water mains have ruptured.		Sheriffs Dept. advises all cities that a state of peril or disaster has *not* yet been declared and all mutual aid will be on a "day to day" basis.
1912½	Mrs. Wilma Thregood, 435 Alpine. She wants to know what she should do, she does not have any electricity or water.		
1914	Natalie Storm, 941 Island View Drive, wants to know what to do, she has no electricity and her street is blocked to all traffic.		
1914½	General Telephone Reports they have emergency crews out attempting to restore any phone service that might have been disrupted by the earthquake.		A unit reports he has been burned by exploding gas tank near Wooley Rd. at Oxnard.
1916	Mr. Louis reports from 401 C Street, the Plaza Vista old folks home, shall we evacuate the building?		
1916½	Dr. Restrue, 200 View Ave., wants to know if he can help, "Where is the emergency medical receiving area?"		
1918	Lt. Clawson, Santa Barbara Police Calls, states his city badly hit by quake, requests mutual aid from surrounding counties and cities — states his mayor has declared a state of local peril!		
1919	Mayor Soohoo: "I want to talk to the watch commander or the person who is in charge of this disaster, I want to know what he is doing about the situation immediately."		
1920	Fire Dept. Dispatcher reports all known fires under control.		Routine Sheriffs dispatch re: disaster
1920½	Mercy Hospital reports they have officer admitted for burn treatment — what shall they do with his badge-gun belt-etc. They don't want to be responsible for firearms at the hospital.		
1922	Lt. Palmer, Ventura PD — They are sending men to Santa Barbara and want to fill their cars — how many men are you sending?		
1923	Edison Co, Mandalay Generating Station reports that all oil storage tanks have ruptured and are leaking into ocean.		
1925	U.S. Coast Guard reports tidal wave off the coast of California — its estimated speed is 400 miles per hr. and its estimated time of arrival is 8 minutes.	Teletype handed to desk. (See end of script).	
1927	Boatmaster, Channel Island Harbor monitors C.G. Radio "What should I do before the tidal wave hits?"		Sheriffs Radio reports tidal wave alert from State Disaster Office.
1929	Mr. R. J. Brodsky reports "The water at the harbor has dropped about 10 feet below normal."		
1930	Curious Citizen, "How bad has the city been hit by the earthquake?"		Unit monitors Sheriffs broadcast is in harbor area — request instructions.
1931	High School Principal, "What should I do about the students attending night school?"		
1932	Edison Co. reports that power will not be restored for 24 hours.		Routine Sheriffs dispatch re: disaster.
1933	Mrs. Hildigard Plentiful, 392 Gonzales Rd. has gone into Labor — needs Dr. — ambulance.		
	END OF SIMULATION		

TELETYPE MESSAGE

Emergency All Points Bulletin for Action By Sheriffs, Chiefs of Police, and Civil Defense Directors of Coastal Counties and Cities: and CHP:

U. S. Coast and Geodetic Survey Reports Probability of Tidal Wave Striking California Coastal Areas. Estimated Time of Arrival Will Follow This Message. Unless Subsequent Bulletins Are Received, Termination of Warning Can Be Assumed Two Hours After ETA of Last Tidal Wave for the Indicated Coastal Location Unless Local Conditions Warrant Continuation of Alert Conditions.

ETA's Are as Follows:

Santa Barbara	1925 Hours PST 3-17-70
Ventura-Oxnard	1927 Hours PST 3-17-70
Santa Monica	1931 Hours PST 3-17-70

H
EMERGENCY CONTROL CENTER MODEL

Large cities often maintain an "Emergency Control Center" which is actually a command post located at police headquarters. The staff positions to man such a unit in a major police department and a plan of its physical layout are presented for clarification.

Emergency Control Center—Functions

The Emergency Control Center shall function as the Department Command Post for serious or major unusual-occurrence control:
1. Provide available services, personnel, equipment, and supplies as requested or as the need arises.
2. Maintain constant communication and coordination with the Field Command Posts.
3. Disseminate pertinent information to the public and news media.

Emergency Control Center—Organization

The Emergency Control Center shall have the following organization:
1. Commander
2. Executive Officer
3. Intelligence Section
4. Personnel Officer
5. Procurement Officer
6. Public Service Station
7. Routing Officer
8. Situation Report Officer
9. Messenger
10. Radio Room

Emergency Control Center Commander—Functions

The Emergency Control Center Commander shall be the duty commander of the Business Office Division. He shall be responsible for the activation, operation, and deactivation of the Emergency Control Center. He shall have line supervision over the personnel assigned to the Emergency Control Center and shall supervise activities from that location.

Executive Officer—Functions

Under the direction of the Emergency Control Center Commander, the Executive Officer shall exercise line supervision over the assigned personnel and the functional operation of the Emergency Control Center. He shall be acting commander of the Emergency Control Center during the absence of the commander.

Intelligence Officer—Functions

The Intelligence Officer shall be responsible for coordination of the activities of the Intelligence Section and shall exercise supervision over the personnel assigned to the Section.

Journal Clerk—Functions

The Journal Clerk shall be responsible for preparation and maintenance of the Emergency Control Center journal and performance of other clerical tasks, as required.

Map Officer—Functions

The Map Officer shall be responsible for posting all maps in the Emergency Control Center, Communications Division, and Public Service Section with pertinent information.

Situation Report Officer—Functions

The Situation Report Officer is responsible for gathering such information as will enable him to have a total cognizance of the unusual occurrence. He shall be prepared to brief authorized personnel, civic officers, and other important persons on pertinent matters relative to the unusual occurrence.

Radio Room Officer—Functions

The Radio Room Officer shall be responsible for the operation of Frequency 9. He shall receive and transmit radio messages and monitor Frequency 9 and any other frequencies being used by Department personnel assigned.

Public Service Section—Functions

The Public Service Section shall have responsibility for the dissemination of information to and reception of information from the public.

Personnel Officer—Functions

The Personnel Officer shall be responsible for the implementation of all requests for personnel required.

Procurement Officer—Functions

The Procurement Officer shall have the responsibility of coordinating the acquisition, assignment, and accounting for the supplies and equipment used or held in reserve during the activation of the Emergency Control Center. He shall be responsible for implementing requests for supplies and equipment.

218   Police Disaster Operations

EMERGENCY CONTROL CENTER ROOM LAY-OUT

- Supply Cabinet
- RADIO ROOM
- MESSENGER WORK AREA
- RADIO CONSOLE
- Situation Report Screen
- Map Screen
- Historian
- Journal Clerk
- Visual Cast
- Visual Cast
- INTELLIGENCE OFFICER ASSISTANT
- ROUTING OFFICER
- PERSONNEL OFFICER ASSISTANT
- PROCUREMENT OFFICER
- Situation Report Officer
- ECC Executive Officer
- ECC Commander
- Duty Deputy Chief
- Auxilary Position
- TELEPHONE TABLE
- OBSERVERS
- Guard
- MAP WALL

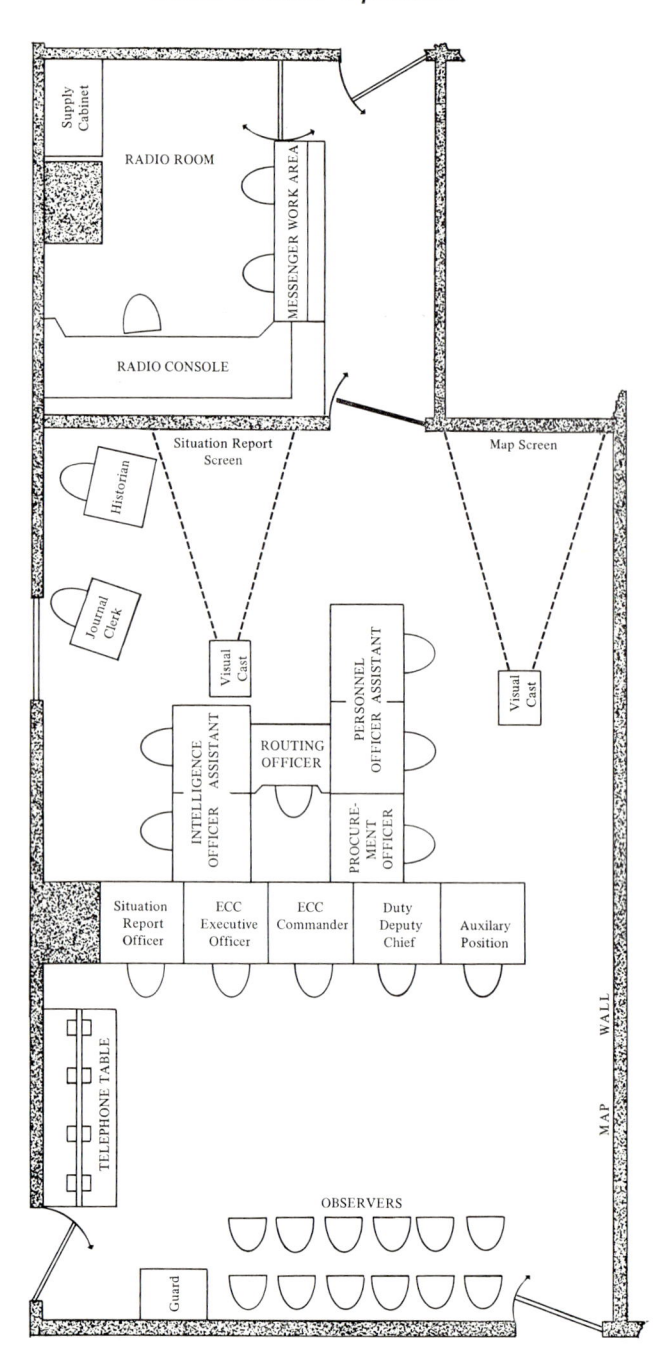

I
DISASTER LOG EXAMPLE

An example of a detailed disaster log is presented to illustrate the type and frequency of entries. This is an actual log but the names, identities, and locations have been omitted to facilitate its use as a case study for classroom discussion. The disaster was caused by the mid-air collision of a military patrol bomber and military transport. The transport fell in the parking lot of a patrol sub-station (precinct) of a large law enforcement agency. The patrol bomber fell in an open area several miles from the sub-station.

LOG SHEET REPORT
STATION–DISASTER LOG–PLANE CRASH

Date _____

7:14 PM Plane exploded and crashed at rear of Station. County Fire Department at scene by 7:25 PM, fighting fire at rear of station, official cars burned.

7:50 PM Car _____ detailed to _____, re: dead body across from location.

8:05 PM Prisoners to _____ Station, by order of _____, A/Lt., Watch Commander.

8:15 PM Car _____ reports a dead female at _____ standing by at location.

8:20 PM Car _____ reports a second plane down with numerous bodies across from the _____.

8:35 PM Chief _____, Inspectors _____, _____, and _____ in station. Captain _____, _____, _____, Sgts. from Hdqtrs D.B. and Capt. _____ in station.

8:35 PM Summation—At the present time:
Eyewitness accounts indicate two planes collided, one crashing at rear of _____ Station parking lot, parts of both planes raining down north and west of station. One plane apparently down in vicinity of _____ with unknown numbers of bodies. Piece of one plane crashed through roof of house at _____, killing a

woman occupant of house. Part of landing gear of plane fell on next street west of _____. Apparently one or the other of the planes was an Air Force plane carrying dependents. Parts of plane hit interview room at rear of detective quarters.

8:45 PM Capt. _____ landed helicopter on _____ School maintenance yard. Standing by.

8:45 PM Colonel _____, Capt. _____, Lt. _____, _____ Air Force base in station. Say they won't be able to establish if this is Air Force plane without tail insignia, etc.

8:45 PM Sigalert put out on 8:05 PM. Inspector _____ requested rebroadcast Sigalert after initial cancellation. Requested expansion of boundaries listed below.

8:45 PM _____ has open line to Hdqtrs. Det. Bureau.
Sgt. _____ reports following Sigalert boundaries:

8:45 PM Salvation Army says food available for 1500 in about one hour.

8:45 PM Crown bus standing by at station.

9:00 PM Officer _____ reports he was contacted by Officer _____ of _____ who stated he found a piece of the wreckage with number 33277, at _____ and _____, above part verified by Colonel _____, _____ Air Station.

9:05 PM Sgt. _____ reports the body of a member of the crew was found in the back yard of _____.

9:05 PM Sgt. _____ reports hot wires down all through area. Dispatcher notified—Edison Co. notified.

9:05 PM Chief _____ reports (phone report from Insp. _____) across from _____ Navy Neptune 127723 has survivors in it, they are now being removed.

9:07 PM Probable survivor at _____.

9:10 PM Local Coroner in Station _____. Instructed to call coroner and get more help.

9:13 PM Tail section wiped out service station across street from _____ Station. No casualties. No fire. North of station, parts found lying at intervals along _____ Street. Air Force notified. Crowd and traffic generally under control except at junction of _____.

9:14 PM Chief _____ en route to _____ Station.

9:25 PM Colonel _____ (Air Force) together with aides and Capt. _____ verified one plane, a C118 with 35 passengers and 5 crew.

Disaster Log Example

9:26 PM   Reserves standing by at following locations where dead bodies located and one damaged house:
Dead Body: _____
Damaged House: _____

9:28 PM   _____ 3 deputies coroners in station equipped to handle 50 bodies.

9:30 PM   _____ has complete record of police cars and private cars damaged in crash. See Supp. report on File _____.

9:31 PM   Auxiliary generator standing by—lights of station out for short period.

9:35 PM   _____, _____ Telephone Company, with mobile unit for our use.

9:35 PM   _____ Emergency has one patient _____, male 23 yrs.—passenger in plane—broken leg. Four doctors standing by and available. _____ Sgts. _____ and _____ rolling to location to question survivor.

9:45 PM   Coroner is going to move bodies from _____ Station to _____ Morgue.

9:46 PM   Dispatcher called stating that one plane was a P2V with 9 aboard and the other a C118 with 35 passengers and 6 crew members.

9:47 PM   Lt. _____ and 15 officers from _____ returning to _____ after rolling on mutual aid.

9:48 PM   Gas tank hit building—tin garage at _____. Reported by Car _____.

9:50 PM   _____ Sgt. and 12 motors logged in at 9:00 PM Standing by.

9:50 PM   Captain _____ reports _____ Coroner ready to move bodies. Colonel _____ (Air Force) indicated approval.

9:55 PM   _____, _____, reports he saw accident from air, got air pictures of scene.

9:57 PM   _____ motors—four motors dispatched at request of Air Force to convoy flat bed truck and other equipment through crowd on _____ from _____.

10:00 PM   _____ reports he has photographs of area at rear of parking lot. Standing by for any additional pictures necessary.

10:02 PM   Report from _____ parts of plane.

10:02 PM   Reports from person at _____ that he has parts of the plane.

10:03 PM   Eyewitness account—See attached sheet _____.

10:04 PM   Eyewitnesses:
_____
_____
_____

10:10 PM   Chief _____ and two officers from _____ PD in station.

10:12 PM   _____ reports wreckage in yard at _____.

10:15 PM Wreckage through roof at _____.
10:20 PM _____ Sgt. _____ and 13 motorcycle officers leaving area. Relieved by Inspector _____.
10:22 PM Salvation Army in station with food for disaster workers.
10:35 PM _____ reports a piece of flesh in vicinity of _____, Det. Sgt. _____ accompanying him to location for investigation—(dead cat).
10:38 PM Parts of plane at _____.
Parts of plane at _____.
10:45 PM State Police reporting area they are blocking:

_____

_____

11:06 PM People who saw plane hit station: _____, _____, _____. Were in _____ restaurant, heard initial blast, ran outside and saw the plane hit station.
11:17 PM _____, _____ Chapter, American Red Cross in station with coffee and doughnuts.

Log continued to accumulate entries at rate of approximately eight per hour until:

6:50 AM _____ reports tank wreckage three houses east of station south side of street on _____.
6:57 AM Sgt. _____ out checking houses on _____ streets from station towards _____ for any possible fatal injuries not reported among civilians.
7:10 AM _____ reports large piece plexiglass, battery and cloth.
7:15 AM Requests from Air Force for Edison Co. to disconnect power at pole in service station.
7:30 AM Car _____ reports 50 shore patrol at scene of Neptune bomber. _____ requests barricades at location to block streets. County road dept. called barricades. Road Dept. en route with barricades from _____.
7:30 AM Edison Co. en route re 7:15 AM requests of Air Force.
7:30 AM State Police reports _____ closed.
7:45 AM _____ called indicating he was taking off with Sgt. _____. Will take aerial photos before setting down at parking lot near _____ Station.
7:55 AM Conversation with Capt. _____ indicates agreement to maintain traffic flow if possible. In charge of operation for State police.
7:57 AM _____ reports 2½ ft. long corrogated hose.

Disaster Log Example

8:00 AM   Air Force requested State Police convoy of long trailer from _____ Air Force Base. Capt. _____ dispatched motors to intercept convoy.
8:04 AM   Sgt. _____ reported check of _____ back of station in house to house check revealed no additional civilian casualties.
8:05 AM   Car _____, _____ detailed up and down _____ posting *no parking* signs.
8:05 AM   Capt. _____ in station on duty.
8:07 AM   _____ coffee shop reports fire extinguisher from plane.
8:07 AM   _____ reports two pieces of metal 3 inches in diameter.
8:20 AM   _____ reports 1½ feet long plywood part of seat.
8:25 AM   Established press log in station to check press in and out upon identification to take daylight pictures of wreckage.
8:29 AM   _____ reports a piece of fan and an oven from Air Force plane.
8:29 AM   Capt. _____ and Sgt. _____ landed helicopter in station parking lot after taking aerial photos.
8:29 AM   _____ reports a large piece of stainless steel, 2½ feet by 4 feet.

Log continued to increase frequency of entries averaging twenty per hour on through the daylight hours. Entries tapered off rapidly by evening but continued at a rate of one or two per hour until the log was ended at 8:20 PM the third day—this log covered a forty-nine-hour period.

J
POLLUTION ALERT SYSTEM

Regulation VII, Emergencies, was adopted on June 20, 1955. It provided for the calling of alerts when any of the following toxic air pollutants reached the following measurements, in parts per million parts of air:

	First Alert	Second Alert	Third Alert
Carbon monoxide	100.0	200.0	300.0
Nitrogen oxides	3.0	5.0	10.0
Sulfur oxides	3.0	5.0	10.0
Ozone	0.5	1.0	1.5

From June 20, 1955 through November 1, 1963, there have been 45 alerts, all First Alerts, and all caused by the ozone readings. There were 15 alerts in 1955, 10 alerts in 1956, one alert in 1957, seven alerts in 1958, four alerts in 1959, two alerts in 1960, two alerts in 1961, one alert in 1962, and three alerts in 1963. Oxides of nitrogen twice have briefly touched alert levels. The highest reading of ozone ever recorded in Los Angeles County was 0.90 part per million parts of air, on September 13, 1955, at the Vernon air monitoring station. In 1956, the highest reading was 0.70 ppm, while a reading of 0.56 ppm at Pasadena on September 26, 1960 is the highest reading since 1956.

The three alert stages are defined in Regulation VII as follows:
1. *First Alert:* Close approach to maximum allowable concentration for the population at large. Still safe but approaching a point where preventive action is required.
2. *Second Alert:* Air contamination level at which a health menace exists in a preliminary stage.
3. *Third Alert:* Air contamination level at which a dangerous health menace exists.

(The contaminants and the levels for each of the three alerts, plus the definitions, where established by a Scientific Committee consisting of public health officials, medical men, chemists, and other scientists.)

Upon declaration of the First Alert, notice goes out to all mass media, to the Sheriff's radio network, Sigalert, Fire Dispatcher, Los Angeles Street Department and Health Department, and others. The public is requested to postpone or curtail any unnecessary driving.

Over direct radio, some 450 industries are directed to prepare to close down should a Second Alert be declared. If it appears that the Second Alert level will be reached, the Control Officer will notify the Emergency Action Committee and the Air Pollution Control Board (Board of Supervisors) and request advice from the Emergency Action Committee. This is a group appointed by the Control Board, comprised of ten members—two experts with scientific training or knowledge in air pollution matters, two licensed physicians, two representatives of industry, two representatives of law enforcement and two representatives of the public at large.

Should a Second Alert stage be reached, with the advice of the Emergency Action Committee, the Control Officer may then order all industries contributing to the contaminant which caused the alert to close down, and may stop all vehicular traffic, except authorized emergency vehicles.

The public again is notified through all mass media. In the event that the Control Officer determines that the public health and safety are in danger, the Emergency Action Committee and the Air Pollution Control Board may take any action authorized by Regulation VII with less than a quorum present.

Should a Third Alert be declared, if it appears that the actions already taken by the Air Pollution Control Officer will be inadequate to cope with the emergency, the Air Pollution Control Board shall request the Governor to declare that a state of emergency exists and to take appropriate actions as set forth in the California Disaster Act.

Upon the termination of any alert, the same people who were notified of its declaration are notified, immediately of its termination.

INDEX

A

Airplane crashes, 89
Air pollution alert system, 122
Ambulance
  coordination, 65
  dispatch post, 65, 125, 130
American Red Cross, 10
Arvin-Tehachapi Earthquake, 145
Avalanches, 93

B

Bakersfield Earthquake, 144
Baldwin Hills Reservoir Burst, 148
Bel-Air Fire, 132
Blizzards, 95
Body recovery, 128
  bag, 70
Boy Scouts, 10

C

California Disaster Office, 9, 127, 167
California Mutual Aid Plan, 159
Carson, California, 5
Casualty sorting, 64
Chemical accident, 98
Civil Aeronautics Board, 91
Civil defense, 7
  actuation, 11
  director, 10
  federal, 7
  law, 11
  local, 9
  police responsibilities, 12
  state, 9
  training, 8, 193
Closed area, 19
Closure, 60
  laws, 35
Coast and Geodetic Survey, 127

Coconut Grove fire, 84
Command Posts, 37
  management, 50
  personnel, 51
Command problems, 73
Community support, 80
Convergence, 47
  control, 95
Coroner, 68, 92
Crescent City, California, 5, 131
Critiques, 76

D

Dam collapses, 101
Dead body recovery, 67
Decontamination, 101
Definitions, 161, 185
Destruction of livestock, 117
Disaster
  commander, 50
  definition, 3
  initial management, 44
  initial phase, 24
  log, 53, 56, 219
  proclamation, 13
  psychology, 78
  simulation, 193, 204
Disaster plan
  duty statements, 20, 25
  legal clarification, 18
  order of succession, 20
  policy statements, 17
  testing, 23, 36

E

Earthquakes, 104
  frequency, 106
  measurement, 107
Electricity blackout, 109
Elizabethport, New Jersey, 5

Emergency
   communications centers, 110
   control center, 134, 215
   operations simulation training, 193
   response plan, 23
Epidemics, 110
Evacuation, 60, 100, 117, 118, 128
   center, 62
   systems, 34
Executive officer, 21
Explosions, 112

F

Family survival training, 30
Federal Aviation Agency, 91
Fires, 114, 132
Flint-Beecher tornado, 48
Floods, 118
Functional change, 22, 183

G

Government loans, 81

H

Hartford, Connecticut, 4
Hilo, Hawaii, 5
Honolulu observatory
Hospital
   communications, 107
   emergency radio, 65
   manpower recall, 67, 136
Hurricanes, 120

I

Identification of the dead, 67
Indiana Fairgrounds Explosion, 83, 142
Indianapolis, Indiana, 5
Intelligence officer, 21, 55, 216
Iroquois theatre fire, 84

J

Joint powers agreement, 175
Journal (log) clerk, 21, 216

L

Land slides, 93
Law enforcement coordinator, 19
Los Angeles, California, 5
Los Angeles Police Tactical Manual, 134, 136

M

Madison River earthquake, 140
Manpower
   log, 53
   pool, 52
   recall alert codes, 29
Map officer, 21, 216
Medical examiner, 68
Mercalli Intensity Scale, 107
Mobile command post, 38
Model disaster plan, 179, 201
Morgue officer, 68
Mutual Aid
   agreements, 16, 33, 171, 175
   assignment, 72
   day to day, 18
   emergency, 19
   problems, 71
   region, 19, 170
   systems, 32

N

National warning system, 193
News releases, 74
New York airplane crash, 136
Nuclear
   accident, 93
   attack, 12
   survival, 8

O

Office of Civil Defense, 193
Operations room simulated, 193
Organizational change in disaster, 183
Organization and function plan, 16, 179

Index

P

Pacoima airplane crash, 135
Panic, 82, 116, 152
  control, 84, 114
  prevention, 85
Personnel officer, 51, 217
Police disaster
  activities, 13
  planning, 16
  response, 12
  role, 14
Pollution, 121
  alert, 224
Post-operational critique, 76
Press
  liaison officer, 54
  notification, 32, 54
  releases, 92
Procurement officer, 217
Property storage, 75
Psychology of victim, 78
Public
  event policing, 86
  safety warnings, 98
  service section, 217

Q

Quarantine, 111

R

Radio room officer, 216
Railroad notification, 130
Recovered
  bodies, 67, 92
  property, 75
Red Cross, 120, 130, 144
Rescue
  debris, 63, 93
  four stages, 64
  intelligence, 63, 93
Reservoir collapses, 101
Resource annex, 36
Richmond, Virginia, 5

Richter scale, 107
Ringling Brothers circus fire, 84

S

Salvation Army, 10, 139, 144
San Fernando, California, 5
Santa Fe train wreck, 146
Seismic sea-wave warning system, 127
Seward, Alaska, 126
Sigalert, 48
Sightseeing, 49
Simulation
  gaming, 184
  room, 195
  scripts, 210
Situation report officer, 22, 216
South Amboy port explosion, 83, 151
Snow drifts, 95
Station command post, 42
Status boards, 57
Systems
  evacuation, 34
  manpower recall, 27
  mutual aid, 32
  notification, 31
  self executing, 27

T

Telephone blackout, 109
Tidal wave, 125, 131
Topanga Canyon fire, 132
Tornadoes, 122
Train wrecks, 128
Triangle Building fire, 84

U

Unit control, 57
University of Southern California, 193

V

Vicksburg, Mississippi, 4

DATE DUE